The World Wide Web Featuring
Netscape Navigator® 4
Software
Illustrated Brief Edition

Donald I. Barker
Chia-Ling H. Barker

COURSE
TECHNOLOGY

ONE MAIN STREET, CAMBRIDGE, MA 02142

an International Thomson Publishing company I(T)P®

Cambridge • Albany • Bonn • Boston • Cincinnati • London • Madrid • Melbourne • Mexico City
New York • Paris • San Francisco • Singapore • Tokyo • Toronto • Washington

The World Wide Web Featuring Netscape Navigator® 4 Software— Illustrated Brief Edition is published by Course Technology

Managing Editor:	Nicole Jones Pinard
Product Managers:	Jeanne Herring, Jennifer Thompson
Production Editors:	Daphne E. Barbas, Catherine G. DiMassa
Development Editor:	Sasha Vodnik
Composition House:	GEX, Inc.
QA Manuscript Reviewers:	John McCarthy, Brian McCooey, Alex White
Text Designer:	Joseph Lee
Cover Designer:	Joseph Lee

© 1998 by Course Technology — I(T)P®

For more information contact:

Course Technology
One Main Street
Cambridge, MA 02142

ITP Europe
Berkshire House 168-173
High Holborn
London WC1V 7AA
England

Nelson ITP, Australia
102 Dodds Street
South Melbourne, 3205
Victoria, Australia

ITP Nelson Canada
1120 Birchmount Road
Scarborough, Ontario
Canada M1K 5G4

International Thomson Editores
Seneca, 53
Colonia Polanco
11560 Mexico D.F. Mexico

ITP GmbH
Königswinterer Strasse 418
53277 Bonn
Germany

ITP Asia
60 Albert Street, #15-01
Albert Complex
Singapore 189969

ITP Japan
Hirakawacho Kyowa Building, 3F
2-2-1 Hirakawacho
Chiyoda-ku, Tokyo 102
Japan

ISBN 0-7600-5953-5

Printed in the United States of America

2 3 4 5 6 7 8 9 B 01 00 99

From the

Illustrated Series™ Team

At Course Technology we believe that technology will transform the way that people teach and learn. We are very excited about bringing you, instructors and students, the most practical and affordable technology-related products available.

▶ The Development Process

Our development process is unparalleled in the educational publishing industry. Every product we create goes through an exacting process of design, development, review, and testing.

Reviewers give us direction and insight that shape our manuscripts and bring them up to the latest standards. Every manuscript is quality tested. Students whose backgrounds match the intended audience work through every keystroke, carefully checking for clarity and pointing out errors in logic and sequence. Together with our own technical reviewers, these testers help us ensure that everything that carries our name is as error-free and easy to use as possible.

▶ The Products

We show both how and why technology is critical to solving problems in the classroom and in whatever field you choose to teach or pursue. Our time-tested, step-by-step instructions provide unparalleled clarity. Examples and applications are chosen and crafted to motivate students.

▶ The Illustrated Series™ Team

The Illustrated Series™ Team is committed to providing you with the most visual introduction to microcomputer applications. No other series of books will get you up to speed faster in today's changing software environment. This book will suit your needs because it was delivered quickly, efficiently, and affordably. In every aspect of business, we rely on a commitment to quality and the use of technology. Each member of the Illustrated Series™ Team contributes to this process. The names of all our team members are listed below.

The Team

Cynthia Anderson	Carol Cram	Jeanne Herring	Art Rotberg
Chia-Ling Barker	David Crocco	Meta Chaya Hirschl	Neil Salkind
Donald Barker	Kim T. M. Crowley	Jane Hosie-Bounar	Gregory Schultz
Ann Barron	Catherine DiMassa	Steven Johnson	Francis Schurgot
David Beskeen	Stan Dobrawa	Mary Kemper	Ann Shaffer
Ann Marie Buconjic	Jennifer Duffy	Bill Lisowski	Christine Spillett
Rachel Bunin	Shelley Dyer	Chet Lyskawa	Dan Swanson
Joan Carey	Linda Eriksen	Karla Mitchell	Marie Swanson
Patrick Carey	Jessica Evans	Tara O'Keefe	Jennifer Thompson
Sheralyn Carroll	Lisa Friedrichsen	Harry Phillips	Sasha Vodnik
Maxine Effenson Chuck	Robin Geller	Nicole Jones Pinard	Jan Weingarten
Brad Conlin	Jeff Goding	Katherine T. Pinard	Christie Williams
Pam Conrad	Michael Halvorson	Kevin Proot	Janet Wilson
Mary-Terese Cozzola	Jamie Harper	Elizabeth Eisner Reding	

Preface

Welcome to *The World Wide Web Featuring Netscape Navigator® 4 Software – Illustrated Brief Edition!* This highly visual book offers new users a hands-on introduction to the World Wide Web and Netscape Navigator and also serves as an excellent reference for future use.

► Organization and Coverage

This text contains four units that cover basic skills necessary for Web browsing. In these units students learn how to use Netscape Navigator 4 software to navigate, search, and explore the Web. This book also contains an appendix that teaches the skills needed to use the Netcaster component of Netscape Navigator 4 software.

► About this Approach

What makes the Illustrated approach so effective at teaching software skills? It's quite simple. Each skill is presented on two facing pages, with the step-by-step instructions on the left page, and large screen illustrations on the right. Students can focus on a single skill without having to turn the page. This unique design makes information extremely accessible and easy to absorb, and provides a great reference for after the course is over. This hands-on approach also makes it ideal for both self-paced or instructor-led classes.

Each lesson, or "information display," contains the following elements:

Each 2-page spread focuses on a single skill.

Concise text that introduces the basic principles discussed in the lesson. Procedures are easier to learn when concepts fit into a framework.

Internet

Using Bookmarks

Netscape Navigator provides a convenient feature called Bookmarks that lets you collect and arrange Web pages of interest in familiar folder-like hierarchies. To add a bookmark, you display the page you want in the document window, click the Bookmark QuickFile button on the Location toolbar, and select the Add Bookmark command on the Bookmark QuickFile menu. The page's name and URL are automatically added to your collection of bookmarks. When your collection of bookmarks grows too large to find page names easily, you can create folders in which to organize them. As marketing manager of The Nut Tree, you think the Exploring business page will be a useful resource once you are ready to put company and product information on the Web. Create a bookmark for this page so you can easily return to it.

Steps

1. Make sure the Exploring business page is displayed in your document window, click the **Bookmarks** button **Bookmarks** on the Location toolbar, then click **Add Bookmark**
   The name and URL of the Exploring business page are added as a bookmark. To see how this works, you will first move to another page, then use the bookmark to return to the Exploring business page.

2. Click the **Home** button
   Your home page appears in the document window.

QuickTip

If the QuickFile list is too long to fit on your screen, you can select the More Bookmarks option at the end of the Bookmark QuickFile menu.

3. Click the **Bookmarks** button **Bookmarks** on the Location toolbar
   The Bookmark QuickFile menu opens, displaying the Add Bookmark, File Bookmark, and Edit Bookmarks options, as shown in Figure B-6. See Table B-3 for a description of these options. Notice that the Personal Toolbar Folder, Guide Sections, and a wide variety of Bookmark folders (e.g., Business Resources, Computers and Technology, Education, Sports) appear beneath these options. By default, your new bookmark appears below the My Stuff folder at the end of the menu.

4. Click the **Exploring business** bookmark
   The Bookmark QuickFile menu closes and the Exploring business page appears.

Trouble?

If you want to keep the bookmarks you save while using someone else's computer, choose the Edit Bookmarks command, select the Save As command on the File menu of the Bookmarks window, specify the drive containing your Student Disk, type a name for the bookmark file in the File name text box, then click Save. Next, to add the saved bookmarks to a bookmark list on your computer, select Import on the File menu of the Bookmarks window and open the file from your Student Disk.

5. Click **Bookmarks** , click **Edit Bookmarks**, scroll down the list if necessary and click the **Exploring business** bookmark, click **Edit** on the menu bar, then click **Delete**
   The bookmark is removed from the list.

6. Click **File** in the menu bar of the Bookmarks window, then click the **Close** command

7. Click the **Home** button to display your home page

► WWW B-10 **NAVIGATING THE WEB**

Tips as well as trouble-shooting advice right where you need it – next to the step itself.

Clear step-by-step directions explain how to complete the specific task, with what students are to type in red. When students follow the numbered steps, they quickly learn how each procedure is performed and what the results will be.

Every lesson features large-size, full-color representations of what the students' screen should look like after completing the numbered steps.

Quickly accessible summaries of key terms, toolbar buttons, or keyboard alternatives connected with the lesson material. Students can refer easily to this information when working on their own projects at a later time.

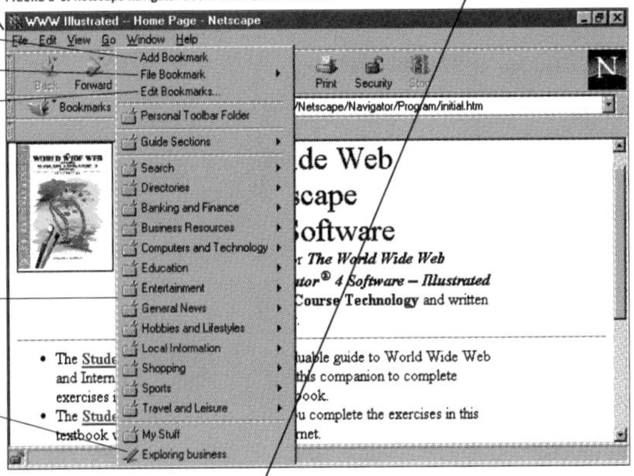

Other Features

The two-page lesson format featured in this book provides the new user with a powerful learning experience. Additionally, this book contains the following features:

▶ **Real-World Skills**
The skills used throughout the textbook are designed to be "real-world" in nature and representative of the kinds of activities that students encounter when working with Netscape Navigator. With a real-world case, the process of solving problems will be more meaningful to students.

▶ **End of Unit Material**
Each unit concludes with a Concepts Review that tests students' understanding of what they learned in the unit. The Concepts Review is followed by a Skills Review, which provides students with additional hands-on practice of the skills they learned in the unit. The Skills Review is followed by Independent Challenges, which pose case problems for students to solve. The Visual Workshops allow students to learn by exploring and to develop critical thinking skills. Students are shown an existing Web page and asked to locate it on the Web.

▶ **Student Offline Companion**
This text includes an innovative Student Offline Companion that lets students complete all the lessons and most of the exercises in this book without accessing the Internet. To use the Offline Companion, Netscape Navigator 4 software is required.

FIGURE B-6: Netscape Navigator Bookmarks QuickFile menu

Add Bookmark
File Bookmark
Edit Bookmarks

Your list may be different

Exploring business bookmark

TABLE B-3: Netscape Navigator Bookmarks window

menu option	description
Add Bookmark	Save the name and address of the current Web page to the Bookmark list
File Bookmark	Specifies a particular Bookmark folder in which to store the bookmark for the current Web page
Edit Bookmarks	Opens the Bookmarks window, which contains options to view, modify, and organize bookmarks using folders and a hierarchical tree structure. For information on how to use these options, check Help in Communicator.

CLUES TO USE

Organizing your bookmarks

As your bookmark list grows, you'll find that organizing the names into categories (e.g., business, education, electronic publishing, entertainment, etc.) makes it easier to locate the page you want to view. Open the Bookmarks window, choose the File menu in the Bookmarks window, click New Folder, type a name for the category (e.g., finance) in the Name text box in the Bookmark Properties dialog box , then click OK. Next, drag and drop the bookmarks into the appropriate folder. Repeat this process for each category until your entire list is organized. To hide or display the bookmarks in a folder, click the minus (–) sign or plus (+) sign.

NAVIGATING THE WEB WWW B-11

Clues to Use boxes provide concise information that either expands on one component of the major lesson skill or describes an independent task that is in some way related to the major lesson skill.

The page numbers are designed like a road map. WWW indicates the World Wide Web section, B indicates the second unit, and 11 indicates the page within the unit.

Instructor's Resource Kit

The Instructor's Resource Kit is Course Technology's way of putting the resources and information needed to teach and learn effectively into your hands. With an integrated array of teaching and learning tools that offer you and your students a broad range of technology-based instructional options, we believe this kit represents the highest quality and most cutting edge resources available to instructors today. Many of these resources are available at www.course.com. The resources available with this book are:

Home Page This book features its own home page, which is provided with the Student Files. The Readme file on the Student Disk contains instructions for installation of the book's home page as the default home page on your browser.

Student Online Companion and Student Offline Companion Also featured with this text are the Student Online Comapanion and the Student Offline Companion. The innovative Online Companion enhances and augments the printed page by bringing students onto the Web for a dynamic and continually updated learning experience. The Offline Companion allows students to work through all the lessons and exercises in the book without Internet access. Instructions for installation of the Offline Companion are in the Readme file that accompanies the Offline Companion files.

Online Instructor's Manual Quality assurance tested and includes:
• Solutions to all lessons and end-of-unit material
• Detailed lecture topics for each unit with teaching tips
• Extra Independent Challenges
• Student Files

WWW.COURSE.COM We encourage students and instructors to visit our Web site at www.course.com to find articles about current teaching and software trends, featured texts, interviews with authors, demos of Course Technology's software, Frequently Asked Questions about our products, and much more. This site is also where you can gain access to the Faculty Online Companion or Student Online Companion for this text.

Course Faculty Online Companion Available at www.course.com, this World Wide Web site offers Course Technology customers a password-protected Faculty Lounge where you can find everything you need to prepare for class including the online Instructor's Manual. Periodically updated items include any updates and revisions to the text and Instructor's Manual, links to other Web sites, and access to student and solution files. This site will continue to evolve throughout the semester. Contact your Customer Service Representative for the site address and password.

Student Files To use this book students must have the Student Files. See the inside front or inside back cover for more information on the Student Files. Adopters of this text are granted the right to post the Student Files on any stand-alone computer or network.

The Illustrated Family of Products

The book that you are holding fits in the Illustrated Series – one series of three in the Illustrated family of products. The other two series are the Illustrated Projects Series and the Illustrated Interactive Series. The Illustrated Projects Series is a supplemental series designed to reinforce the skills learned in any skills-based book through the creation of meaningful and engaging projects. The Illustrated Interactive Series is a line of computer-based training multimedia products that offer the novice user a quick and interactive learning experience. All three series are committed to providing you with the most visual and enriching instructional materials.

Contents

 ► [**Internet**]

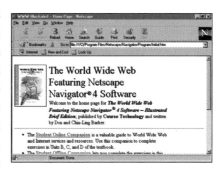

Contents

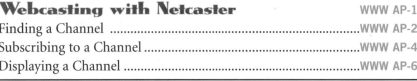

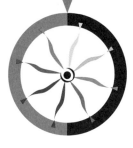

Getting

Started with the World Wide Web

Objectives

► **Understand Netscape Navigator**
► **Start Netscape Navigator 4**
► **Explore the Netscape Navigator window**
► **Work with menus and toolbars**
► **Move around a Web page**
► **Find text**
► **Get Help**
► **Print a Web page**
► **Exit Netscape Navigator**

The lessons in this unit introduce you to the World Wide Web and Netscape Navigator, which let you access the World Wide Web. In this book, you assume the role of a newly hired marketing manager for The Nut Tree, a fictitious catalog company that sells confectioneries and assorted nuts in attractive custom gift packaging. You will use Netscape Navigator software to explore how to establish a presence on the World Wide Web in order to help your company expand its business. Begin by exploring the World Wide Web and the Netscape Navigator environment.

Understanding Netscape Navigator

Netscape Navigator 4 is a software program known as a **Web browser** that lets you interact with the World Wide Web. The **World Wide Web** (also known as the Web, WWW, and W3) is a vast series of electronic documents called **Web pages** or **Web documents** that are linked together over the Internet. The **Internet** is a collection of networks that connects computers all over the world. A **network** consists of two or more computers that are connected to share data. The Internet connects millions of computers using a combination of phone lines, coaxial cables, fiber-optic cables, satellites, and other telecommunications media, as depicted in Figure A-1. Netscape Navigator 4 allows you to find, load, view, and interact with Web pages. Web pages typically incorporate both text and graphics, as shown in Figure A-2, however, they may include multimedia such as sound and video clips too. ◄──── As the marketing manager for The Nut Tree, you recognize the many ways you could use Netscape Navigator to make your company more successful. With a Web browser you can:

 Navigate the Web, to view and interact with the Web pages of other companies to see how they are marketing their products on the Web.

 Search the Web, using effective and efficient strategies, to find information that will be useful as you plan your online marketing campaign for The Nut Tree Company.

 Explore the Web, to examine some of the major categories of information on the Web and to learn more about the issues important to Web users.

 Subscribe to Netcaster channels, to automatically receive personalized, dynamic, and timely multimedia content delivered directly to your computer at periodic intervals (see the Appendix "Webcasting with Netcaster" for information on Netcaster).

Netscape Communicator

Netscape Navigator 4 is also available as a component of Netscape Communicator 4, a suite of products that includes Netscape Navigator 4, plus Composer (an easy to use editor for creating your own Web pages), Messenger (a full-featured e-mail program that lets you send and receive messages), Collabra (a newsgroup reader that provides public or private discussion forums), Conference (a real-time audio communication program that allows you to speak with another person over the Internet or within an intranet), and an array of products to enhance group productivity. This book assumes that you are using the standalone version of Netscape Navigator 4. To learn more about Netscape Communicator or Netscape Navigator, you can visit www.netscape.com.

FIGURE A-1: Structure of the Internet

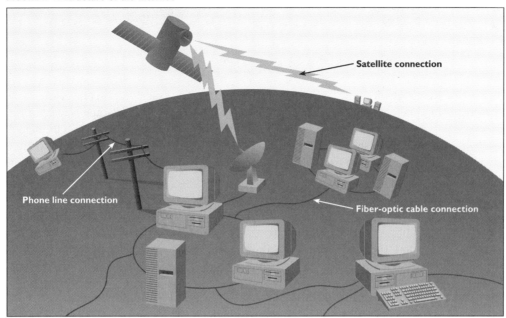

FIGURE A-2: Sample World Wide Web page

Understanding intranets

An **intranet** uses the same communication technology as the Internet but access is restricted to only the members of a particular group or organization. Intranets offer companies many advantages, such as additional security beyond what is available on the Internet, inexpensive and easier installation and maintenance than traditional information systems, and the same familiar Web browser interface people are already using to access information on the Internet. As a consequence, corporate America is rushing to implement intranets throughout their information infrastructure.

Starting Netscape Navigator 4

In this lesson you will start Netscape Navigator. The exact location of Netscape Navigator may vary on different computers. Hence, the steps you take to start Netscape Navigator might be different than those given below. See your instructor or technical support person for help if you are unable to locate the Netscape Navigator program. ✏ Before you can plan ways to market The Nut Tree's products on the Web, you need to launch Netscape Navigator and explore its features.

1. Click the Start button on the taskbar

The Start menu opens in the lower left corner of your screen.

2. Point to the Programs command on the Start menu

A second, or cascade, menu opens listing the programs available on your computer.

3. Point to Netscape Navigator on the Programs menu

A third cascade menu opens displaying the applications in Navigator, as shown in Figure A-3.

4. Click the Netscape Navigator command

Netscape Navigator launches and displays *The World Wide Web Featuring Netscape Navigator 4 Software—Illustrated Brief Edition* home page, as shown in Figure A-4. The home page is the first Web page Netscape Navigator loads when you launch the program.

Trouble?

If the Netscape Navigator page shown is different from the one in Figure A-4 or if you are prompted for a user profile, ask your instructor or technical support person for assistance.

FIGURE A-3: Cascade menu showing the Netscape Navigator components

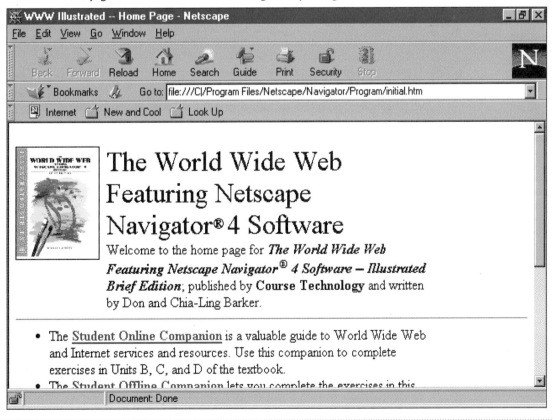

Netscape Navigator command

FIGURE A-4: Home page for *The World Wide Web Featuring Netscape Navigator 4 Software—Illustrated Brief Edition*

WWW Illustrated -- Home Page - Netscape

File   Edit   View   Go   Window   Help

Back   Forward   Reload   Home   Search   Guide   Print   Security   Stop

Bookmarks   Go to: file:///C|/Program Files/Netscape/Navigator/Program/initial.htm

Internet   New and Cool   Look Up

The World Wide Web Featuring Netscape Navigator® 4 Software

Welcome to the home page for ***The World Wide Web Featuring Netscape Navigator® 4 Software – Illustrated Brief Edition***; published by **Course Technology** and written by Don and Chia-Ling Barker.

- The <u>Student Online Companion</u> is a valuable guide to World Wide Web and Internet services and resources. Use this companion to complete exercises in Units B, C, and D of the textbook.
- The <u>Student Offline Companion</u> lets you complete the exercises in this

Document: Done

Internet

Exploring the Netscape Navigator Window

When you start Netscape Navigator, the Netscape Navigator application window opens. The screen elements enable you to enter, view, and search for information. Begin your first day on the job at The Nut Tree by exploring the Netscape Navigator environment. Using Figure A-5 as your reference, locate each of the following window elements on your screen:

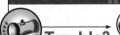

Trouble?

If your Netscape program window does not cover your entire desktop, click the Maximize button.

 A **Web page**, or **Web document**, is a specially formatted file designed for use on the World Wide Web. It lets you show information to anyone using the Web. A Web page typically includes text, graphics, and links, which you select to connect to other Web pages. A Web page might also include sound and video clips that you can access if your computer has the appropriate hardware and software. The **title bar** displays the title of the current Web page.

 The **menu bar** displays the names of the menus that contain Netscape Navigator commands. When you click the name of a menu on the menu bar, Netscape Navigator displays a list of commands from which you can choose.

 The **toolbars** (**Navigation**, **Location**, and **Personal**) contain icons that act as shortcuts to activate frequently used menu commands.

 The **Location text box**, on the Location toolbar, displays the address of the current page shown in the document window. A **Web address**, or **Uniform Resource Locator (URL)**, is a unique string of text that identifies the location of a Web page on the World Wide Web.

The **status indicator** (the Netscape Communications corporate logo) animates as a new page is loading. When the status indicator stops moving, the page-loading process is complete.

The **vertical and horizontal scroll bars** let you move quickly through a page. The scroll box in each scroll bar indicates your relative position on the page. You may see both, one, or neither of the scroll bars depending on the dimensions of the page you are viewing.

The **progress bar** displays important information about the current operation, such as the percentage of a Web page layout and graphical display that has loaded so far. The lower-left box in the progress bar visually indicates the status of the page-loading process by sliding a bar back and forth.

FIGURE A-5: Elements of the Netscape Navigator program window

Security indicator

Status indicator

Title bar

Menu bar

Navigation toolbar

Location toolbar

Personal toolbar

Web address or URL

Web page

Location text box

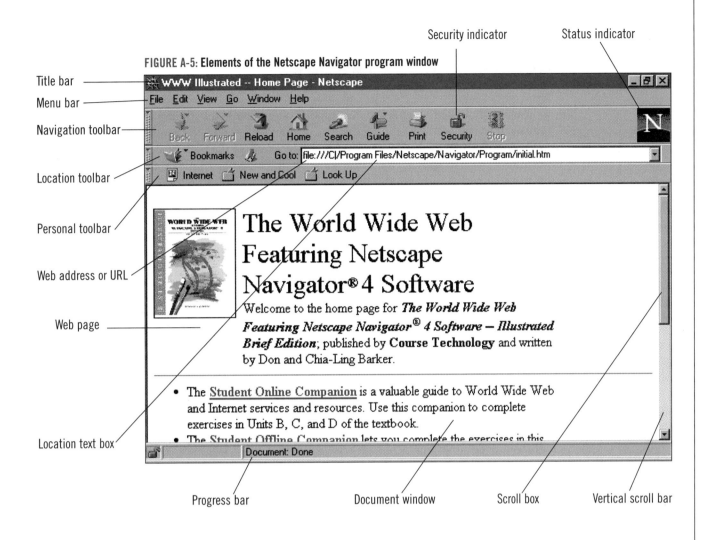

Progress bar

Document window

Scroll box

Vertical scroll bar

Working with Menus and Toolbars

Netscape Navigator often provides several ways to complete the same task using menus and its toolbars. Although the menus in Netscape Navigator contain the available commands and options, the toolbars, shown in Figure A-6, offer a quicker and easier way to access frequently used commands. Table A-1 provides a brief description of the buttons on the **Navigation** and **Location** toolbars. You can use the Netscape Navigator menu and toolbar buttons to browse for more information on the World Wide Web. Familiarize yourself with them to learn how they can help you work more efficiently as you market The Nut Tree products online.

QuickTip

Click the list arrow, on the right side of the Location text box, to display the names of the pages you have recently visited. To revisit a page, simply click it on the list.

QuickTip

You can add buttons to the Personal toolbar containing Internet shortcuts to your favorite Web sites. For details on how to customize the Personal toolbar, click Help on the menu bar, click Help Contents, click the Index button, then scroll down the left frame and select "toolbar buttons."

1. **Click View on the menu bar, then click the Reload command**
   Since your home page hasn't changed, the document window loads and displays the same page, as shown in Figure A-7. Although in this instance, the page appears the same, reloading a Web page is an important capability to ensure you are seeing the most recent version. This is because Navigator saves pages you visit in a file on your computer, called a **cache**, to reduce loading time. However, the content on the Web is continually changing and using reload guarantees that you are viewing the most up-to-date information.

2. **Click the Reload button on the Navigation toolbar**
   Notice that during reloading, the Netscape logo is animated. When it stops, the page has been sucessfully reloaded.

3. **Click once more, but this time, quickly click the Stop button before the home page finishes reloading**
   If you are quick enough, the home page appears without graphics or other page elements. The Stop button is a convenient way to halt the lengthy loading process of a page laden with images and other large elements. You will use it often when accessing the Web over a slow Internet connection such as a modem connection.

CLUES TO USE

Altering the appearance of toolbars

To reorder the toolbars, drag a toolbar by the tab on its left side to one of the three possible toolbar positions at the top of the window. To hide a toolbar, position the pointer over the toolbar's tab, then click the tab. The toolbar will **collapse**, or become hidden.

When a toolbar is collapsed, its tab appears below the remaining toolbars shown. To display a toolbar, simply move the pointer over its tab the pointer shape changes to a hand, then click the tab. The toolbar expands to display its available options.

FIGURE A-6: **Netscape Navigator toolbars**

Navigation toolbar
Location toolbar
Personal toolbar

FIGURE A-7: **Home page**

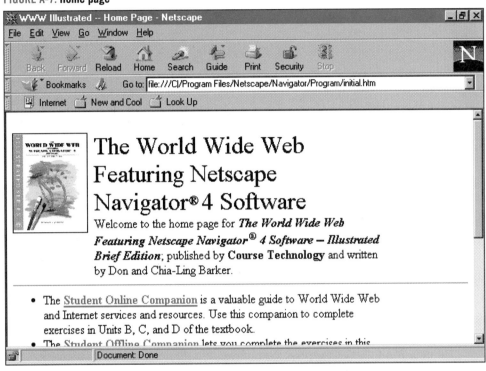

TABLE A-1: **Navigation and Location toolbar options**

button	description	button	description
Back	Displays previous page	Print	Allows the printing of the current Web page
Forward	Displays the next page in the series of pages already viewed	Security	Displays information about secured documents; remains grayed out for unsecured documents
Reload	Forces Netscape Navigator to completely reload a page	Stop	Halts the page-loading process
Home	Displays your home (opening) page	Bookmarks	Displays a menu of favorite Web sites from which to choose
Search	Allows searching of the Web based on key word(s)	Location:	The Page Proxy icon (located to the left of the Location text box) creates a button or icon pointing at the current URL displayed in the Location text box. For information on how to use the Page Proxy icon, open the Help contents window, click the Index button, scroll down to "toolbars" in the left frame and select it, then choose "Using the Location Toolbar."
Guide	Displays a list of new, cool destinations, people, and software on the Web		

Internet

Moving Around a Web Page

Netscape Navigator provides several convenient methods to scroll through longer pages. Although it is considered wise to keep Web pages short and concise for easy browsing, you will occasionally encounter long pages (e.g., directories, articles, etc.). Table A-2 summarizes the ways you can move through a Web page. ▰ Practice moving through your home page, using a combination of these methods.

Steps

1. Click the **scroll down arrow** at the bottom of the vertical scroll bar
   The document window scrolls down several lines in the home page to reveal new information at the bottom of the window.

2. Click the **scroll up arrow** at the top of the vertical scroll bar
   The document window scrolls up several lines in the page.

3. Click below the **scroll box** in the vertical scroll bar
   The document window scrolls down the length of one window to display the next portion of your home page, stopping at the bottom if less than one window of information remains.

4. Click above the **scroll box** in the vertical scroll bar
   The document window scrolls up the length of one window, or back to the top in a short page, to show the previous view of the page.

5. Drag the **scroll box** to the bottom of the vertical scroll bar
   The document window displays the bottom of the page, as shown in Figure A-8. Notice the scroll box has moved to the bottom of the vertical scroll bar, indicating you have reached the end of the current Web page.

6. Drag the **scroll box** to the top of the vertical scroll bar
   The document window displays the top of the page.

7. Press **[Ctrl][End]**
   The bottom of the page appears in your document window.

8. Press **[Ctrl][Home]**
   The top of the page appears in the document window.

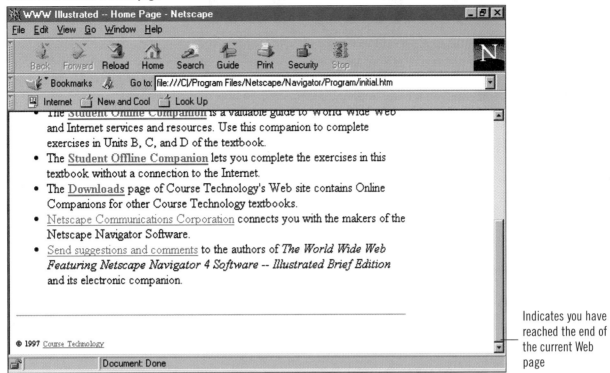

Indicates you have reached the end of the current Web page

TABLE A-2: **Methods for moving through a Web page**

to move	click or press
Down several lines	Down arrow in the vertical scroll bar or press ↓
Up several lines	Up arrow in vertical scroll bar or press ↑
Down one window	Below the scroll box in the vertical scroll bar or press [PgDn]
Up one window	Above the scroll box in the vertical scroll bar or press [PgUp]
To the top of the Web page	[Ctrl][Home]
To the bottom of the Web page	[Ctrl][End]

Internet

Finding Text

Sometimes you will want to find a specific word or phrase in a Web page. Scrolling through the page and trying to spot text can be a very haphazard and time-consuming process. Netscape Navigator provides a Find in Page command on the Edit menu to automate this process. You are searching for information on how to market products on the Web, so use the Find button to search the Web page for occurrences of the word "Web."

1. Make sure your home page is open, click **Edit** on the menu bar, then click the **Find in Page command**

The Find dialog box opens, as shown in Figure A-9. Table A-3 lists all the Find dialog box options.

2. Click the **Find what text box** and type **Web**

The word "Web" appears in the text box.

3. Click **Find Next** in the dialog box

The document window changes to show the portion of the page containing the first instance of "Web." You may need to reposition the Find dialog box to see the first instance of "Web" highlighted on the Web page.

4. Click **Find Next** again in the dialog box

The second occurrence of "Web" in this page appears highlighted in the document window.

5. Click **Find Next** once more

Yet another instance of "Web" is found.

6. Continue to click **Next** until you receive the message "Search String Not Found!", then click **OK** in the dialog box

Netscape Navigator has now searched the entire page from top to bottom.

7. Click **Cancel** to close the Find dialog box

The last instance of "Web" remains highlighted after closing the Find dialog box.

QuickTip

When repeatedly searching for the same word or phrase in a document, you can press the F3 key, with the Find dialog box closed, to locate the next instance of the search string.

FIGURE A-9: Find dialog box

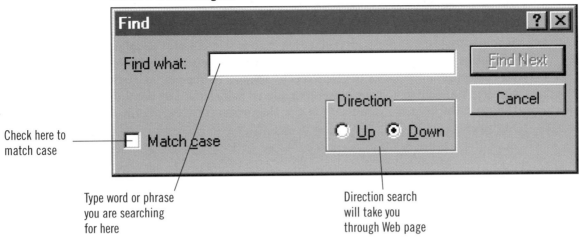

Check here to match case

Type word or phrase you are searching for here

Direction search will take you through Web page

TABLE A-3: Find dialog box options

option	description
Find what text box	Allows the entry of keywords to search for
Find Next button	Locates and highlights the next occurrence of text in a Web page that matches the entry in the Find what text box
Cancel button	Closes the Find dialog box
Match case check box	When selected, causes Netscape Navigator to search for text that exactly matches the capitalization used in the Find what text box
Up option button	Searches the Web page from the insertion point up for a match to the entry in the Find what text box
Down option button	Searches the Web page from the insertion point down for a match to the entry in the Find what text box

Getting Help

Netscape Navigator includes an online Help system that can provide information and instructions on its features and commands while you are using Netscape Navigator. Table A-4 describes the commands available on the Help menu. ➤ As the new marketing manager for The Nut Tree, you want to find out what information is available to help users of Netscape Navigator. Use the Help Contents command on the Help menu to view information about Netscape Navigator.

Steps 1234

1. **Click Help on the menu bar**
   The Help menu opens.

QuickTip

To locate a topic in the Help contents, scroll the list in the left menu of the NetHelp window and click the desired topic. The right portion of the window changes to display information on the topic.

2. **Click Help Contents**
   The Netscape Navigator NetHelp window opens, as shown in Figure A-10. Note that the NetHelp window is divided into two sections. The left border is a menu controlling what is displayed in the right portion of the window. The left menu contains three major options: Contents, Index, and Find. The Help topic links appearing below these icons automatically change depending on the icon selected. For example, clicking the Contents icon causes the topic links on the left and the contents on the right to display information specifically related to the Contents selection.

Trouble?

If an error dialog box appears when you select a Help command, it is probably because you are not currently connected to the Internet. Although the Help Contents, Index, and Find function are available offline (locally), many of the other commands on the Help menu require being online (i.e., being connected to the Internet).

3. **Click the Navigator Help icon or click the Browsing the Web link**
   Information describing how to use Netscape Navigator for viewing the Web appears in the right portion of the NetHelp window, as shown in Figure A-11. Notice that the left side of the document window displays a list of links with topics related to viewing the Web with Navigator.

4. **Scroll down the list of topics to briefly see what information is available**

5. **When you are done looking at the topics, click the Close button in the upper-right corner of the NetHelp window to close it**
   Navigator appears on your desktop with your home page displayed in the document window.

FIGURE A-10: **Netscape Navigator Help**

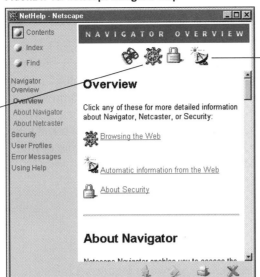

Navigator Help icon ——

Icons for information on the Navigator components

FIGURE A-11: **Viewing the Internet page in NetHelp**

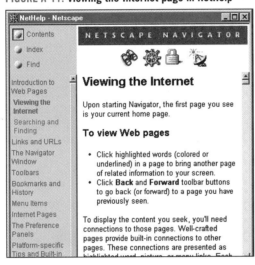

TABLE A-4: **Descriptions of the Help Menu Commands**

command	provides
Help Contents	Local list of help topics, index, and a keyword(s) find feature
Release Notes	Latest information on Netscape Navigator
Product Information and Support	Instructions on how to register and get support for your copy of Netscape Navigator
Software Updates	Information and procedures on upgrading Netscape software
Register Now	Allows the registration of your copy of Netscape Navigator
Member Services	Configuration and other information for Navigator
International Users	Information on using Netscape Navigator in different languages and from outside the U.S.
Security	Information on the security scheme used in Netscape Navigator
About Plug-ins	Information about Netscape Navigator plug-ins
About Font Displayers	Shows your present font (i.e., character shapes) selections and allows additions and deletions of font formats
About Navigator...	Version and copyright information

Internet

Internet

Printing a Web Page

You can print the current Web page (i.e., the one displayed in your document window) by simply selecting the Print button on the toolbar, specifying the print options you want in the Print dialog box, and clicking the OK button. The Print dialog box lets you specify the number of copies and the page ranges you want to print. Table A-5 provides additional information on all the Netscape Navigator printing options. ◢◤ Melissa Shea, the owner of The Nut Tree, has never used the Internet or the World Wide Web. She has asked to see a printout of what a home page looks like. Use the Print dialog box to print two copies of your home page—one for Melissa and one for your records.

QuickTip

You can use the Print Preview command on the File menu to look at a picture of what the current document will look like when printed. The Print Preview window also lets you zoom in on portions of the document for closer examination. You can print right from the Print Preview window by clicking the Print button.

1. Click **File** on the menu bar, then click **Print**

The Print dialog box opens, as shown in Figure A-12.

2. Double-click the **Number of copies text box**, then type **2**

The Print dialog box is now set to print two copies. If you accidentally entered a different number of copies, repeat Step 2 to correct the mistake. (Note: This number of copies becomes the default number to print until you either exit Netscape Navigator or change the number.)

3. Make sure your printer is turned on, ready to print, and contains paper

A paper printout, or hardcopy, of the company's home page is ready to be printed. The quality and speed of the printout depends on the type of printer. (Color printers are typically slower but have the advantage of producing hard copy that closely resembles the appearance of a Web page on screen.)

4. Click **OK**

The Print dialog box closes and the current Web page prints.

Trouble?

If you are not connected to a printer or the printer fails to print, ask your technical support person or instructor for assistance.

FIGURE A-12: **Print dialog box**

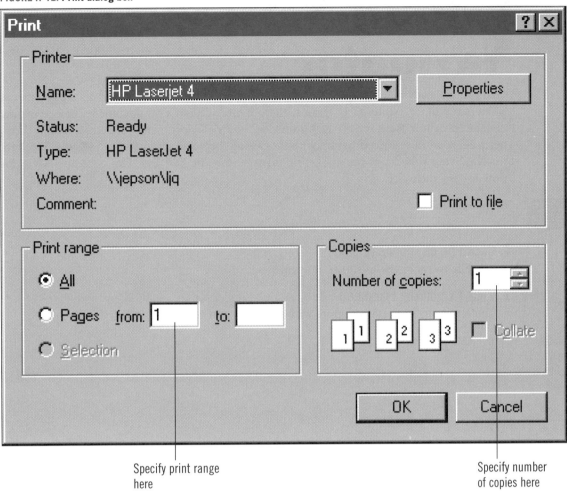

Specify print range
here

Specify number
of copies here

TABLE A-5: **Printing options**

options	description
Printer	Displays information about the active printer *Name* indicates printer to use *Status* reveals the readiness of the printer *Type* displays the brand and model of active printer *Where* shows the destination of the print job *Comment* displays available information on printing *Properties* provides access to the settings of the active printer *Print to file* sends a print job to a file instead of a printer
Print range	Indicates the pages to print *All* prints the entire document *Pages* prints the pages you specify *Selection* prints selected portions of the document
Copies	Indicates the number and order of copies to print *Number of copies* specifies how many copies to print *Collate* prints multiple copies of the document in sequence

Internet

Exiting Netscape Navigator

When you are ready to exit Netscape Navigator, you select the Exit command on the File menu. Unlike many other Windows programs, there is no need to save documents before exiting Netscape Navigator. Netscape Navigator only lets you view documents, not create or edit them. Therefore, you can exit the program without closing the document window. ➤ You have completed your first day as the marketing manager for The Nut Tree. Exit Netscape Navigator before leaving the office.

1. **Click File on the menu bar**
   The File menu opens, as shown in Figure A-13.

2. **Click Exit on the File menu**
   The Netscape Navigator program window closes and you return to Windows.

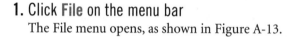

QuickTip

You can also exit from Netscape Navigator by clicking the Close button in the top right corner of the title bar of the Netscape Navigator application window.

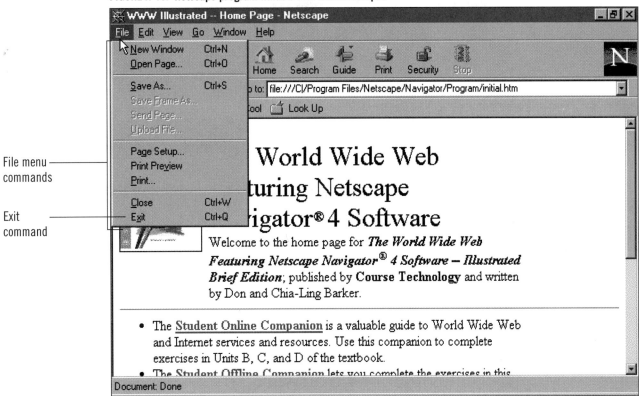

File menu commands

Exit command

Opening, switching, and closing multiple instances of Netscape Navigator

You can use the New command on the File menu to display a cascade menu and choose the Navigator Window command to open another instance of the Netscape Navigator program. Use either the Taskbar in Windows 95/NT or the Window command in Navigator to switch between the different instances of Navigator. This feature lets you view multiple Web pages simultaneously. If you want to close one of the Web pages without closing the others, choose the Close command on the File menu of the page you want to close. To close all open pages at once, simply select Exit from the File menu of any Netscape Navigator program window.

Internet

Practice

► Concepts Review

Label each of the elements of the Netscape Navigator program window in Figure A-14.

FIGURE A-14

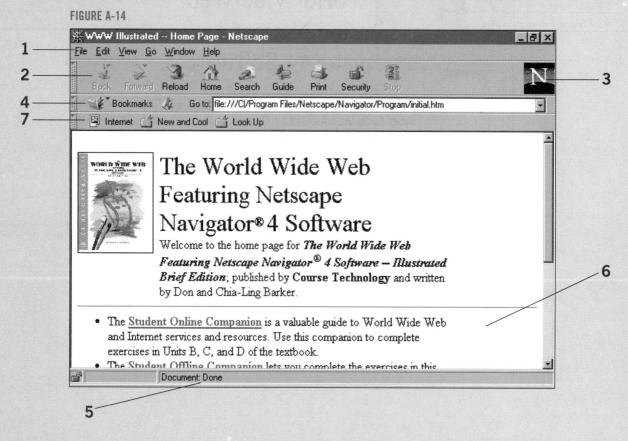

Match each of the terms below with the statement that best describes its function.

8. **Toolbar**
9. **Scroll bar**
10. **Document window**
11. **Location text box**
12. **Status indicator**

a. Displays a Web page
b. Indicates Netscape Navigator is loading a page
c. Contains shortcuts to menu commands
d. Indicates the address of the current page
e. Contains controls for moving through a document

Select the best answer from the list of choices.

13. **Which is NOT an option on the Window menu?**
    a. Explorer
    b. History
    c. Netcaster
    d. Bookmarks

14. A Web browser lets you
  a. Create Web pages.
  b. Explore binary files on your hard disk.
  c. View pages on the Web.
  d. Browse non-ASCII files at remote sites.

15. To view another part of a Web page
  a. Click the Relocate button on the toolbar.
  b. Move the scroll box in the scroll bar.
  c. Drag the toolbar.
  d. Select the Leap command from the Navigate menu.

16. To go to the top of a document
  a. Drag the scroll box to the top of the scroll bar.
  b. Press [Ctrl][Top].
  c. Click the Home button on the toolbar.
  d. Double-click the scroll bar.

17. To find words in a Web page
  a. Click the Find button.
  b. Press [CTRL][L].
  c. Click the Find in Page command on the Edit menu.
  d. Double-click the Location toolbar.

18. You can get Netscape Navigator Help by
  a. Clicking Help on the menu bar.
  b. Pressing the [F2] key.
  c. Clicking the Help button on the toolbar.
  d. Pressing [Alt][Help].

19. What key(s) do you press to move down a Web page?
  a. [End]
  b. [PgDn]
  c. [Shift][End]
  d. [Enter][End]

20. You can print a document in Netscape Navigator in any of the following ways except
  a. Click the Print button on the toolbar.
  b. Click File, click Print, then click OK.
  c. Click File, click Print Preview, then click Print.
  d. Press [Alt][P] and then [Enter].

21. The Navigation toolbar lets you do all of the following except
  a. Print a Web page.
  b. Search the Web.
  c. See what's new.
  d. See a list of favorite Web sites.

22. **Your home page is**
    a. A Web page detailing information about your computer.
    b. The initial Web page Netscape loads whenever you launch the program.
    c. A page you create to end your Web presentation.
    d. A Web page devoted to the realty business.

23. **URL stands for**
    a. Universal Requester List.
    b. Uniform Resource List.
    c. Uniform Resource Locator.
    d. Universal Regional Locator.

24. **You can exit Netscape Navigator by**
    a. Double-clicking Netscape Navigator's Close button.
    b. Clicking Exit on the File menu.
    c. [Alt][F], [X].
    d. All of the above.

 # Skills Review

1. **Start Netscape Navigator and identify elements of the program window.**
    a. Make sure the computer is on and Windows is running.
    b. Click the Start button, then point to Programs.
    c. Click Netscape Navigator.
    d. Without referring to the lesson material, identify the toolbars, the menu bar, the scroll bars, the location text box, the status indicator, and the progress bar in the Netscape Navigator program window.

2. **Explore the Netscape Navigator menus and toolbars.**
    a. Click the Guide button on the Navigation toolbar. A Web page appears with a list of resources that include Yellow Pages, People, Netsearch, What's New and What's Cool, and Netscape In-Box Direct.
    b. Select the Yellow Pages resource. A Web page appears from which you can access businesses all over the world. Scroll down the page and check out the listings.
    c. When you are done, click the Home button on the Navigation toolbar to return to your default page.

3. **Move around the document window.**
    a. Click the scroll down arrow in the vertical scroll bar twice.
    b. Click the scroll up arrow in the vertical scroll bar twice.
    c. Click below the scroll box in the vertical scroll bar.
    d. Click above the scroll box in the vertical scroll bar.
    e. Drag the scroll box to the bottom of the vertical scroll bar.

4. Find text.

a. Click the Find in Page command on the Edit menu to open the Find dialog box.

b. Use the dialog box to locate how many times the word "Netscape" appears in your home page.

c. Double-check your results by searching the document again using the Up option button in the Direction area of the Find dialog box.

d. Close the Find dialog box.

5. Explore Netscape Navigator Help.

a. Click Help on the menu bar.

b. Click the Help Contents command on the Help menu.

c. Click the Index icon and look for information on using the Help menu.

d. When you finish, close the NetHelp window.

6. Print a Web page.

a. Click the Security command on the Help menu.

b. When the Security page finishes loading in the document window, click File on the menu bar, then click Print.

c. To print just the first page of this Web document, click the Pages option button in the Print range area of the Print dialog box.

d. Press [Tab] and type "1" in the "to" text box, then click OK.

7. Preview a Web page, then print the page and exit Netscape Navigator.

a. Click the Home button.

b. To see how the current Web page will look when printed, click File and then click Print Preview. Netscape formats the document for printing and displays it. When a Web page is longer than a single printed page, click the Next Page button at the top of the Print Preview window to display another page. The Zoom In and Zoom Out buttons allow you to examine in detail any portion of a Web page.

c. Click the Print button, then click OK to print the Web page. (The Close button returns you to the document window without printing the Web page.)

d. When the page is printed, click File on the menu bar, then click Exit.

▶ Independent Challenges

1. Write a short essay on what you hope to learn from this book. Be sure to include a section on how you think Netscape Navigator and the World Wide Web will help you in your academic/professional life. You can use any word processor to write and print this essay. If you are unfamiliar with a word processor, use Notepad, a simple text processor included with Microsoft Windows in the Accessories program group.

2. Use your library to find several articles on how the World Wide Web might impact businesses. Write a brief summary of the articles. You can use any word processor to write and print the summary. If you are unfamiliar with a word processor, use Notepad, a simple text processor included with Microsoft Windows in the Accessories program group.

Internet

▶ Visual Workshop

Use the skills you learned in this unit to display the "About User Profiles" topic in the NetHelp window, as shown in Figure A-15. Print a copy of the page.

FIGURE A-15

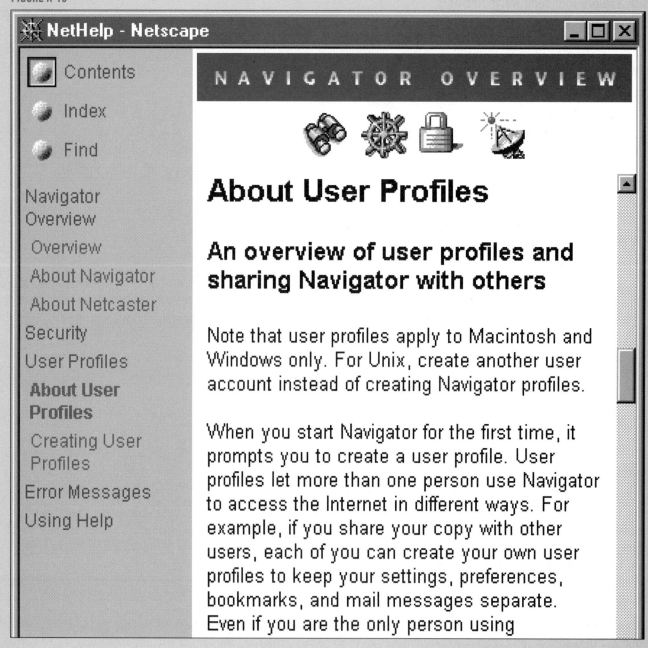

Navigating
the Web

Objectives

► **Understand hypertext links and URLs**
► **Find, start, and stop links**
► **Move backward and forward**
► **View history**
► **Use Bookmarks**
► **Work with frames**
► **Take a guided tour**
► **Enter a URL address**

Now that you are familiar with Netscape Navigator's toolbars, menus, dialog boxes, and Help system, you are ready to navigate the Web. In this unit, you will learn how easy it is to move between Web pages. Netscape Navigator provides a powerful set of tools that let you control what you view on the World Wide Web. ➤ As the marketing manager for The Nut Tree, you firmly believe that the Web represents an attractive medium for marketing the firm's products. However, before making any recommendations to Melissa Shea, the owner of the company, you want to become adept at moving around the Web.

Internet

Understanding Hypertext Links and URLs

Think of the World Wide Web as a very large book or encyclopedia of information. Each page in this encyclopedia is referred to as a **Web page**. Each page in this encyclopedia may contain one or more hypertext links. **Hypertext links, hyperlinks,** or just **links,** enable you to open related Web pages by clicking them with your mouse. You can use these links to follow a topic from page to page through the encyclopedia without regard to where or in what order the pages reside. To distinguish links from the other text in a Web page, links are highlighted in a special color and underlined. Figure B-1 shows a Web page featuring links to food retailers. If you wanted to find information on companies selling gift packages of assorted nuts and confectioneries, you could scroll down the page and examine the various store descriptions. When you located a shop of interest, you could simply click on the hypertext link and your Web browser would locate and load the indicated Web page using its **URL,** or **Uniform Resource Locator.** Using the encyclopedia analogy, a Web page's URL would be equivalent to its page number. For example, the URL address for the Web page shown in Figure B-1 is http://www.internet-mall.com/index.html. Each Web page has a URL, which serves as its address within the World Wide Web. There are several components that make up a URL. Each of these components is described in detail below.

 The acronym HTTP (HyperText Transfer Protocol) is found in each URL. **HTTP** is the communication standard, or **protocol**, established for the World Wide Web. It ensures that different computers are communicating in the same language when sending and receiving Web pages.

 A colon and two forward slashes (e.g., http://) indicate that the Web page is located on a remote Web site.

 A Web site, or server, is a computer or a network of computers that makes pages available on the Web. The name of a Web site typically begins with the three letters "www" (e.g., www.internet-mall.com), signifying that the location is part of the World Wide Web. The second part of the site name (e.g., internet-mall.com) is called the **domain name**. The first component of the domain name (e.g., internet-mall) usually stands for the name of the institution that owns the site. The final three letters, the **global domain** (e.g., .com), tell you the kind of site or institution you are dealing with. In this example, .com indicates that this is a commercial site. Table B-1 briefly describes the current global domain extensions.

FIGURE B-1: Hypertext links in Web pages

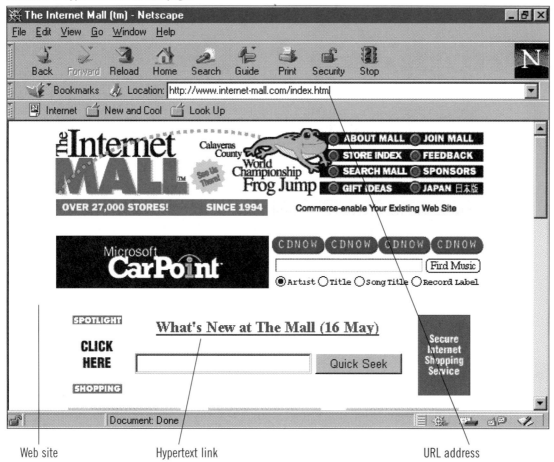

Web site   Hypertext link   URL address

TABLE B-1: Global domains

global domain	description
.com	Commercial sites
.edu	Educational institutions
.mil	Military
.net	Network organizations
.org	Not for Profit organizations
.gov	Government agencies, departments, and institutions

Graphical hypertext links

Links to other Web pages also appear as graphics. Certain graphics, or **imagemaps**, in a Web page contain regions, or links, to other Web pages. For example, a Web page might display a picture of a solar system with nine planets. Each planet could be a graphical link that, when clicked, would open a page with information about that planet. Since these graphical links are easy to understand, you'll find that many Web sites use imagemaps to simplify navigation.

Finding, Starting, and Stopping Links

To make links easily recognizable, they are always highlighted in a color different from the rest of the text on a Web page. Once you select a link, it changes color again to indicate that you have chosen it. Unselected, or unfollowed, links are blue by default, while links that have already been selected, or followed, are purple. By changing the color of a link, Netscape Navigator provides a clear marker to help you keep track of where you have been on the World Wide Web. Note that the link color setting can be changed on individual computers, however, and thus links may not always appear in the default colors. To select a link in a Web page, simply click it. Netscape Navigator will then attempt to locate and load (open) the page using its URL address. However, because the Web runs over the Internet, with thousands of sites connected by thousands of networks, things can go wrong when you try to load a page. If your browser seems to be taking a very long time to locate and/or load a page, you can interrupt the operation by clicking the Stop button on the toolbar. This will halt the loading operation and return control of the browser to you. Netscape Navigator will continue to display the current page in the document window up to the point when a new page begins loading. If you have selected the Stop button, the document window will display the portion of the page Navigator was able to load before the load operation was halted. ▰▰▰ Begin your quest for information on how other companies use the Web as a marketing tool by selecting a link from your home page.

QuickTip

If you are using the Student Offline Companion, read the Clues to Use box on p.B-5.

Trouble?

If your home page does not contain the link <u>Student Online Companion</u>, check with your instructor or technical support person.

1. **Start Netscape Navigator and scroll through your home page until you locate the link <u>Student Online Companion</u>; or, if you are working offline, locate the <u>Student Offline Companion</u> link, then position the mouse pointer over the link**
   Notice that when you move the mouse pointer over the link, the shape changes from an arrow ⌖ to a hand 👆 shape. This is yet another indication that this is a hypertext link

2. **Click the <u>Student Online Companion</u> link or the <u>Student Offline Companion</u> link**
   After a moment, the status indicator stops moving and the document window displays the Student Online Companion, as shown in Figure B-2. This page provides an extensive guide to sites on the Web and is designed for you to use with your textbook. You want to select a link from this page that will lead you to Web pages providing information on other companies selling products and services on the Web.

3. **Scroll through the Web page until you reach the heading Explore the Web, then click the link <u>Exploring business</u>, which is part of this section**
   A new Web page opens, displaying a short list of links of topics on the page.

4. **Click the link <u>Virtual Malls</u> indented under the link <u>Shopping</u>**
   The page will automatically scroll down to the beginning of the Malls section of the page, which features links and descriptions of various virtual shopping malls on the Web.

5. **Scroll down to the <u>Internet Mall</u> link, click it, then as the new Web page begins to load, click the Stop button 🛑 on the Command toolbar**
   Netscape Navigator halts the process of finding and loading the linked page. If you click the Stop button too soon, your document window may be empty. Just click the Reload button on the toolbar to restart the loading process and wait until the page begins to appear before clicking the Stop button. If you receive an error message, click OK and try this step again.

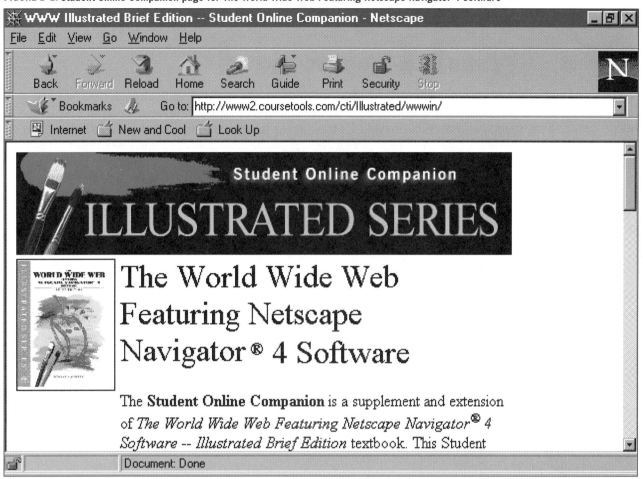

Tips for users of the Student Offline Companion

If you are using the Student Offline Companion with this text, you are working with Web pages that are stored on your local drive or network rather than on the Internet. The Student Offline Companion contains the Web pages you need in order to complete all of the lessons and most of the end-of-unit exercises in Units B, C, and D. In order to keep the Offline Companion to a reasonable size, only those links that are necessary to complete the lessons or exercises will be active on each Web page that you load. Because it is designed to simulate the experience of working online, the heading on the Offline Companion home page says "Student Online Companion."

The pages you are working with are located on a local disk drive. Therefore your screens will differ from those in the book in that the Location box will show a local drive address (beginning with "file:///") for each Web page you load, rather than an HTTP address

(beginning with "http://"). For instance, in Figure B-2, the address shown for users of the Offline Companion will be **file:///cl/offline/course/index.htm** (or a similar address beginning with "file:///") rather than the URL shown above.

In addition, the URL addresses you are instructed to type in steps in the book will be different if you are using the Student Offline Companion. In the lessons, alternative addresses will be provided for Offline Companion users; for end-of-unit exercises, your instructor can supply you with replacement addresses for those sites to which you will need access. However, it is recommended that the end-of-unit exercises be completed online rather than offline in order for you to gain experience actually working on the Internet and to thoroughly explore the resources available on the World Wide Web.

Internet

Moving Backward and Forward

Netscape Navigator makes it easy to navigate backward and forward through Web pages you have previously viewed. Selecting the Back button on the toolbar displays the previous page you visited in your document window. Choosing the Forward button sends you to the next page in the series of pages you have been viewing. Melissa Shea was impressed by the list of virtual malls you found in the previous lesson. Now that you see how widely the Web is used by other companies as a marketing tool, you need to find out how to put The Nut Tree company and product information onto the Web. Use the Back and Forward buttons to return to the Student Online Companion page to look for another link that may provide the information you are looking for.

Steps

1. **Click the Back button** on the Navigation toolbar once
   The previously viewed page displays in your document window.

2. **Click the Back button** until it grays out
   Your home page displays in the document window. The Back button is now grayed out to indicate that you have reached the first page viewed and that this button is temporarily unavailable for use. See Figure B-3.

3. **Click the Forward button** once
   The Student Online Companion page appears, as shown in Figure B-4. Notice that the Back and Forward buttons are not grayed out, and that the page is scrolled down to show the link that you originally clicked to exit the page.

QuickTip

When the Back or Forward button is available, you can click and hold down either button to display a list of pages previously visited, letting you instantly jump to a page without the necessity of clicking through the intervening pages.

FIGURE B-3: Your home page

The Back button is grayed out to indicate it is inactive

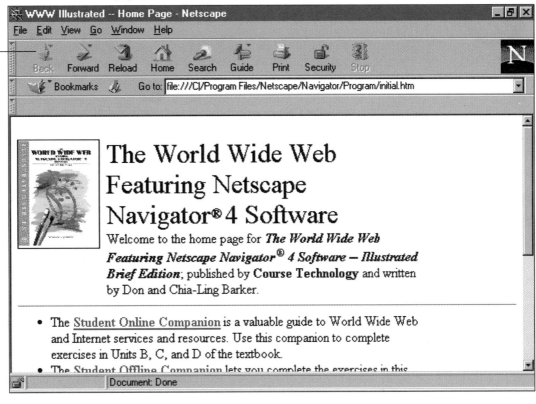

FIGURE B-4: Student Online Companion page

Back and Forward buttons are both active

Link that was originally used

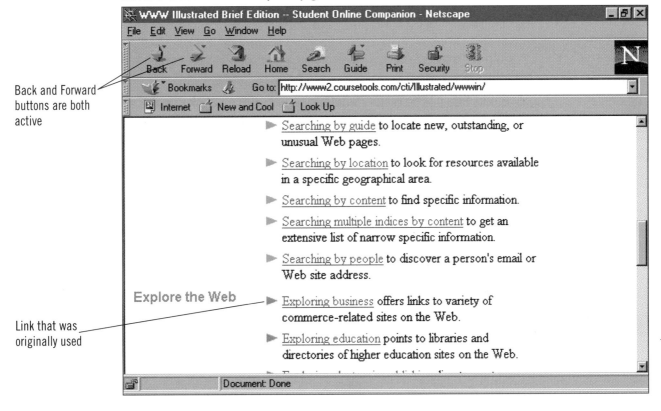

Internet

Viewing History

Netscape Navigator offers another way to move among previously selected Web pages with its History command. Instead of using the Back and Forward buttons to search for a previously viewed page, you can go straight to it by selecting History on the Window menu and then selecting the name of any previously viewed page. ◄▬▬ Use the History command to review the Web pages you have already visited to make sure you didn't overlook anything of value.

Steps

QuickTip

To sort a history list, click the button above the column you want to use to reorder the information. Clicking the Title button once sorts the listings in ascending order; twice sorts in descending order.

QuickTip

To instantly load a previously viewed page from the History list, double-click it.

1. Click **Window** on the menu bar, then click **History**

A History window opens, as shown in Figure B-5. If other Web pages have been viewed recently with your browser, your list may be considerably longer than the one pictured in the figure. The name of the most recent page viewed appears at the top of the list. This list runs from the most recent to the oldest viewed page at the bottom. Table B-2 provides a brief description of the information available in the History window.

2. Click **Exploring business** in the Title column

The row of information for the Exploring business Web page is highlighted.

3. Click **File** on the menu bar of the History window, then select **Go to Page**

The History window minimizes to an icon on the taskbar and the document window changes to display the Exploring business Web page viewed previously.

4. Click the **History icon** on the Windows taskbar

The History dialog box restores to its former size. You can use the options in the menu bar to perform extensive searches and sorts of the history list. (Refer to the Navigator Help facility for further information on using these menus.) For now, you decide to close the History window.

5. Select **File** on the History window menu bar, then click **Close**

The History window closes.

FIGURE B-5: History window

FIGURE B-5: History window

Menu bar —

Button bar —

History list area —

Title	Location	First Visited	Last Visited	Expiration	Visit Co...
WWW Illustrated -- ...	http://www2.coursetools....	Less than on...	Less than on...	5/26/1997 1...	3
WWW Illustrated -- ...	FILE:///C|/PROGRAM FI...	Less than on...	Less than on...	5/26/1997 1...	2
Exploring business	http://www2.coursetools....	Less than on...	Less than on...	5/26/1997 1...	2
Exploring business	http://www2.coursetools....	Less than on...	Less than on...	5/26/1997 1...	2
The Internet Mall (tm)	http://www.internet-mall.c..	Less than on...	Less than on...	5/26/1997 1...	1

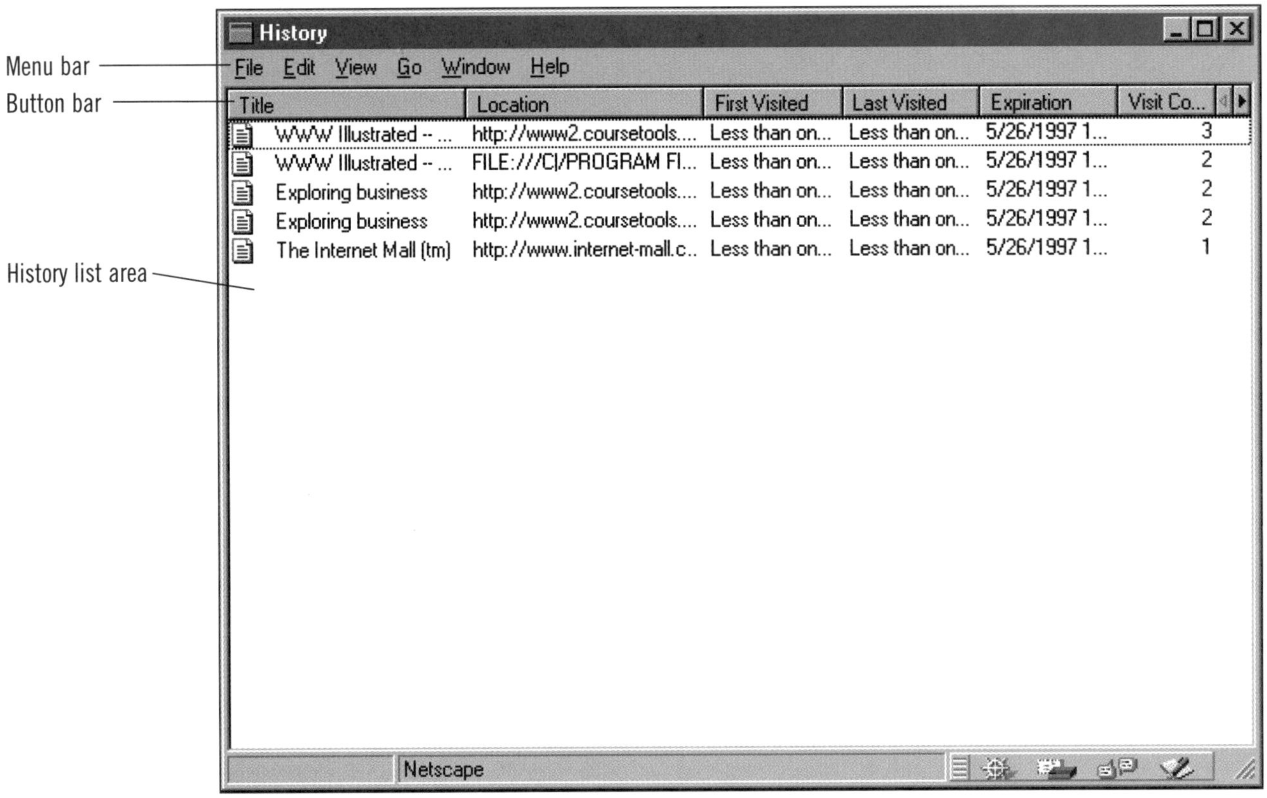

TABLE B-2: Description of the history list in the History window

column	description
Title	Displays the name of visited pages
Location	Shows the URL of visited pages
First Visited	Displays the date the page was first visited
Last Visited	Shows the date the page was last visited
Expires	Indicates how long the page visited information is to be stored
Visit Count	Displays the number of times the page has been visited.

Internet

Using Bookmarks

Netscape Navigator provides a convenient feature called Bookmarks that lets you collect and arrange Web pages of interest in familiar folder-like hierarchies. To add a bookmark, you display the page you want in the document window, click the Bookmark QuickFile button on the Location toolbar, and select the Add Bookmark command on the Bookmark QuickFile menu. The page's name and URL are automatically added to your collection of bookmarks. When your collection of bookmarks grows too large to find page names easily, you can create folders in which to organize them. ⬤➤ As marketing manager of The Nut Tree, you think the Exploring business page will be a useful resource once you are ready to put company and product information on the Web. Create a bookmark for this page so you can easily return to it.

1. Make sure the Exploring business page is displayed in your document window, click the **Bookmarks button** 🕊️ʸ Bookmarks on the Location toolbar, then click **Add Bookmark**
   The name and URL of the Exploring business page are added as a bookmark. To see how this works, you will first move to another page, then use the bookmark to return to the Exploring business page.

2. Click the **Home button** 🏠
   Your home page appears in the document window.

3. Click the **Bookmarks button** 🕊️ʸ Bookmarks on the Location toolbar
   The Bookmark QuickFile menu opens, displaying the Add Bookmark, File Bookmark, and Edit Bookmarks options, as shown in Figure B-6. See Table B-3 for a description of these options. Notice that the Personal Toolbar Folder, Guide Sections, and a wide variety of Bookmark folders (e.g., Business Resources, Computers and Technology, Education, Sports) appear beneath these options. By default, your new bookmark appears below the My Stuff folder at the end of the menu.

4. Click the **Exploring business** bookmark
   The Bookmark QuickFile menu closes and the Exploring business page appears.

5. Click 🕊️ʸ Bookmarks , click **Edit Bookmarks**, scroll down the list if necessary and click the **Exploring business** bookmark, click **Edit** on the menu bar, then click **Delete**
   The bookmark is removed from the list.

6. Click **File** in the menu bar of the Bookmarks window, then click the **Close** command

7. Click the **Home button** 🏠 to display your home page

QuickTip

If the QuickFile list is too long to fit on your screen, you can select the More Bookmarks option at the end of the Bookmark QuickFile menu.

Trouble?

If you want to keep the bookmarks you save while using someone else's computer, choose the Edit Bookmarks command, select the Save As command on the File menu of the Bookmarks window, specify the drive containing your Student Disk, type a name for the bookmark file in the File name text box, then click Save. Next, to add the saved bookmarks to a bookmark list on your computer, select Import on the File menu of the Bookmarks window and open the file from your Student Disk.

FIGURE B-6: Netscape Navigator Bookmarks QuickFile menu

Add Bookmark

File Bookmark

Edit Bookmarks

Your list may be different

Exploring business bookmark

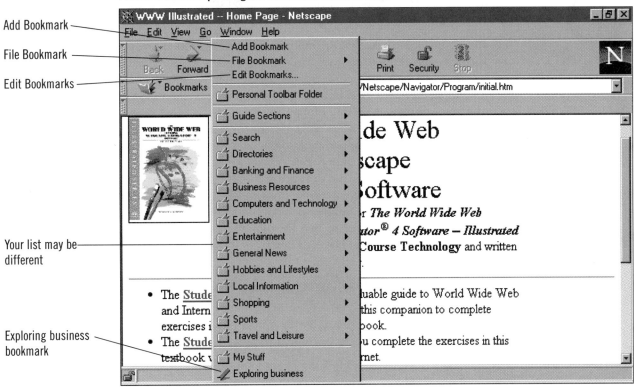

TABLE B-3: Netscape Navigator Bookmarks window

menu option	description
Add Bookmark	Save the name and address of the current Web page to the Bookmark list
File Bookmark	Specifies a particular Bookmark folder in which to store the bookmark for the current Web page
Edit Bookmarks	Opens the Bookmarks window, which contains options to view, modify, and organize bookmarks using folders and a hierarchical tree structure. For information on how to use these options, check Help in Communicator.

Organizing your bookmarks

As your bookmark list grows, you'll find that organizing the names into categories (e.g., business, education, electronic publishing, entertainment, etc.) makes it easier to locate the page you want to view. Open the Bookmarks window, choose the File menu in the Bookmarks window, click New Folder, type a name for the category (e.g., finance) in the Name text box in the Bookmark Properties dialog box , then click OK. Next, drag and drop the bookmarks into the appropriate folder. Repeat this process for each category until your entire list is organized. To hide or display the bookmarks in a folder, click the minus (–) sign or plus (+) sign.

Working with Frames

Netscape Navigator lets you display multiple windows or **frames** within your document window. This convenient feature allows the document window to be divided into numerous frames, each containing its own unique information. For example, if the document window is divided into two frames, the major links from the initial page are placed in the left frame as menu items. The right frame displays the results of selections made in the left frame. In other words, the left frame lists menu choices that, when clicked, cause the selected item to appear in the right frame. The left frame contents remain constant, so that you are free to make other menu selections. If you want to go back or forward in a specific frame, just click the frame, and use the standard Back and Forward buttons on the Command toolbar. Table B-5 provides a list of additional right mouse commands that are available from within a frame when pointing at text. Frames sound like a useful feature to incorporate into The Nut Tree's Web documents. Familiarize yourself with frames so that you can discuss them with Melissa and make recommendations for how they should be used in the company's Web pages.

Steps

1. Select the <u>**Student Online Companion**</u> link or the <u>**Student Offline Companion**</u> link on your home page
   The Student Online Companion for the World Wide Web Featuring Netscape Navigator 4 Software page appears in your document window.

2. Scroll down the page and click the <u>**Frame version of this Student Online Companion**</u> link under the Netscape Updates heading
   Your document window changes to display the Student Online Companion divided into two frames, as shown in Figure B-7. The left frame contains a list of items you can choose to view.

3. Click the link <u>**Exploring the Web**</u> in the left frame, then click the link <u>**Exploring education**</u>
   The right frame displays the Exploring education Web page.

4. To move back one frame on the right, click the right frame, then click the **Back button** on the Command toolbar (You could also right-click the frame and select the Back command)
   The right frame changes to show the information previously displayed before you made your selection in the left frame.

5. To move forward a frame, click the right frame, then click the **Forward button** on the Command toolbar (or right-click the frame and choose the Forward command from the pop-up menu)
   The right frame again displays the Exploring education Web page information.

6. Click the **Home button** to return to your home page

QuickTip

If you right-click on an image in a frame, instead of text, you will be presented with an entirely different menu of commands than those shown in Table B-5. The new commands are designed to work with an image. The same holds true if you right-click on a link in a frame. The menu you see will contain commands specific for working with hypertext links. (For more information on frames and right-click command sets, see the Help Contents on the Help menu.)

FIGURE B-7: Student Online Companion rearranged using frames

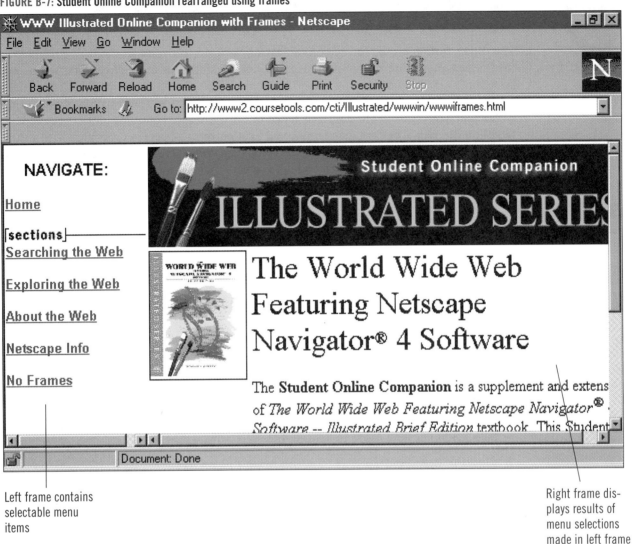

Left frame contains
selectable menu
items

Right frame dis-
plays results of
menu selections
made in left frame

TABLE B-5: Right mouse button commands available when pointing to text in a frame

command	description
Open Frame in New Window	Displays frame contents in a document window
Back	Moves back one frame
Forward	Moves forward one frame
Reload Frame	Refreshes the current frame with the latest information from the Web site
Stop	Terminates the frame loading process
View Frame Source	Displays window with the code used to create the frame
View Frame Info	Shows information about the frame (e.g., Netsite location and date last modified)
Add Bookmark	Adds the link to your bookmarks
Create Shortcut	Creates a desktop icon that automatically displays the page associated with the current link when double-clicked
Send Page	Allows the address of the current frame to be sent in an e-mail message

Internet

Taking a Guided Tour

The **Guide button** on the Navigation toolbar of Navigator provides an excellent guidepost to the Internet, plus a directory of people on the Net, a listing of business directories, and menus pointing to new and outstanding sites to visit on the Web. Guided tours of Web resources can save you a lot of time in finding information to fit your needs (as you'll learn more about in Unit C "Searching by Guide"). The guides included in Navigator focus on some of the more popular topics on the Web. They are maintained, and kept current, by people experienced with these areas of interest. ✎ Melissa wants the company's Web site to be up-to-date with the latest sites on the Web. She asks you to take a look at what is new on the Web.

Steps

QuickTip

If you are using the Student Offline Companion, replace Steps 1 and 2 with the following:
1. Click the Student Offline Companion link on your home page, then click the Frames Version of this Student Online Companion link.
2. Click the link Netscape Info in the left frame, then click the link What's New. Resume with Step 3.

1. Click and hold the **Guide button** on the Navigation toolbar until a drop-down menu opens, then release the button
The drop-down menu displays a list of options, as shown in Figure B-8.

2. Click the **What's New** command
The What's New page appears listing some new sites on the Web, as shown in Figure B-9.

3. Scroll down the list and click the link for a site that looks interesting
The home page for the site loads.

4. Explore the page, then use the **Back button** to return to the new site listings and select another new place to visit on the Web

5. Click the **Home button** to return to your home page
Your home page appears in the document window.

FIGURE B-8: Guide button's drop-down menu

Netscape guide to
the Internet by
Yahoo!

Searchable list of
people on the Net

Directories of
businesses on
the Web

Newest Web
arrivals

Outstanding sites,
interesting starting
points from which
to explore the Web

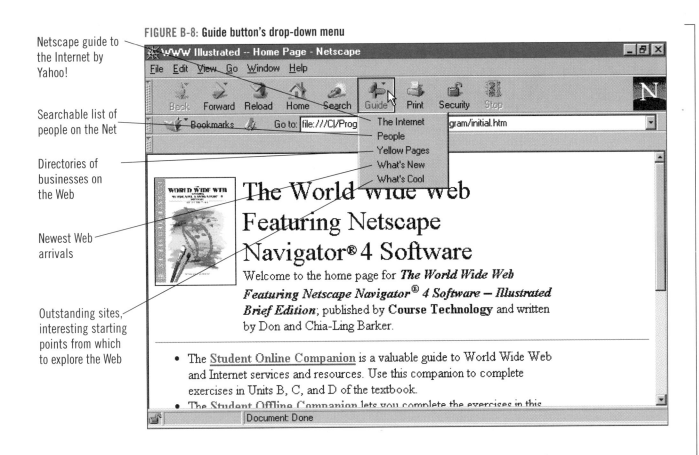

FIGURE B-9: What's New page

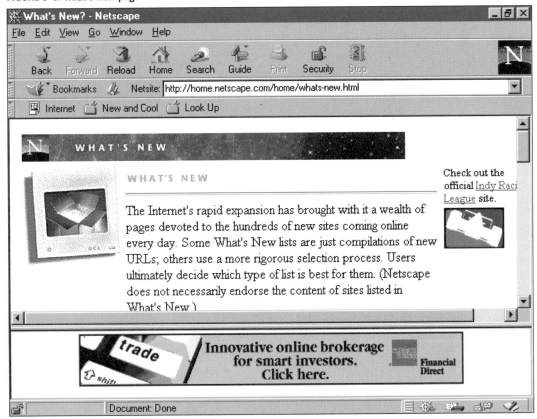

Internet

Entering a URL Address

Links make navigating the Web as simple as pointing and clicking. However, when you want to view a page without a readily available link, you will need to manually enter the location of the page, which is its URL. You manually enter an URL address in the Location text box on the Location toolbar in Netscape Navigator. 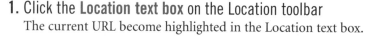 Your marketing assistant found a list of Web sites for popular specialty food items in a magazine. She made a list of the company names and URLs (shown in Table B-6) to provide ideas for The Nut Tree Company home page. Use the URL address for Chocolate Rampage, to view the firm's Web page.

Steps

Trouble?

If you are using the Offline Companion, the "Cl/Offline/" in the address represents one possible disk drive and folder location for the Offline Companion files. Your instructor or technical support person may provide you with an alternative drive and folder in order to complete these steps.

1. **Click the Location text box on the Location toolbar**
   The current URL become highlighted in the Location text box.

2. **Type http://www.fishnet.net/~chocolate in the Location text box; or, if you are using the Student Offline Companion, type file:///Cl/Offline/fishnet/index.htm**
   The old URL disappears and the name of the text box changes to Go to as you type the new URL, as shown in Figure B-10.

3. **Once you have typed the new URL, press [Enter]**
   The status indicator animates, and after a brief time the Chocolate Rampage Web page appears, as pictured in Figure B-11. (If you receive an error while trying to open the Chocolate Rampage page, enter another URL listed in Table B-6.) The Go to text box reverts to the Location text box, unless the typed URL only contains a domain name (e.g., www.netscape.com), in which case the Netsite text box appears, indicating the URL is pointing to the Net site itself, not to a directory or filename within the site.

4. **Explore the page, then click the Location text box on the Location toolbar again**
   The textbox still displays the URL you entered earlier. You can use your edit keys to modify this address rather than typing in an entire new URL.

5. **Click at the end of the previous URL address in the Location text box**
   A flashing insertion point (text cursor) appears at the end of the URL.

6. **Press [Backspace] as many times as necessary to erase everything after http://www. or, if you are using the Student Offline Companion, after file:///Cl/Offline/**
   The Go to text box now displays only the beginning of a URL address, http://www.

QuickTip

To save time, type a URL without the "http://" portion of the Web address and Navigator will automatically fill in "http://" to load the page. Also, for a super shortcut, if the URL is in the form "http://www.<one word>.com," you can type merely the one word. For instance, if you wish to go to "http://www.yahoo.com" you can type "yahoo" and Navigator will fill in "http://www." and ".com" for you after you press Enter.

7. **Type godiva.com/ and press [Enter] or, if you are using the Student Offline Companion, type godiva/index.htm and press [Enter]**
   Once more the status indicator animates and, after a brief time, the document window displays the initial page at the Godiva Chocolatier company.

8. **Click the Home button 🏠 on the Navigation toolbar**
   The document window displays your home page.

9. **Exit Netscape Navigator**

FIGURE B-10: Entering a URL manually

Partially-typed URL

Go to text box

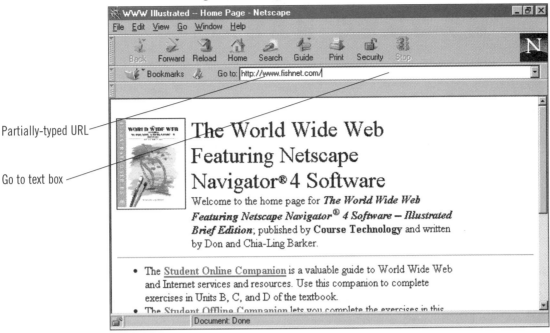

FIGURE B-11: The home page for Chocolate Rampage

TABLE B-6: URLs of potential competitors of The Nut Tree

company name	url
Chocolate Rampage	http://www.fishnet.net/~chocolate
A Chocolaty Chocolate Factory	http://www.LongGrove.com/
Ann Hemyng Candy's Chocolate Factory	http://mmink.com/mmink/dossiers/choco.html
North Dakota 24K Karamels	http://www.minot.com/~karamels/karamels.htm
Rowena's	http://emall.com/Rowena/Rowena1.html

Practice

► Concepts Review

Label the elements of the Web address and the Location toolbar shown in Figure B-12.

FIGURE B-12

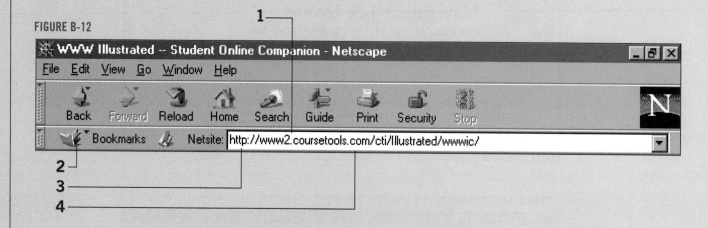

Match each of the terms below with the statement that best describes its function.

5. Add Bookmark
6. Forward button
7. URL
8. Home button
9. Back button
10. History

a. Returns you to your home page
b. Loads the previously viewed page
c. Records the name and location of a Web page
d. Jumps to the next page in a previously viewed series of pages
e. "Address" of a Web page
f. Displays Web pages visited recently

Select the best answer from the list of choices.

11. A link in a Web page lets you
   a. Jump to another Web page.
   b. Connect two hyper-zones.
   c. Load a paper page.
   d. Create linkages that never fail.

12. To view the previous page
   a. Click the Hyper Reverse button.
   b. Click the Back button.
   c. Click the Previous command on the Go menu.
   d. Select the Backup command on the Go menu.

13. The Bookmark QuickFile menu lets you do everything except
   a. Add the current page to the bookmark list.
   b. Store the current page to a folder.
   c. Open the Bookmarks window.
   d. Move a page around the Web.

14. The History window lets you do everything except
   a. Sort the History list based on page title.
   b. Search for a particular page previously viewed.
   c. Create a hypertext link.
   d. View a page previously visited.

15. Which URL address is incorrect?
   a. http://www.company.com
   b. http://www.company.com/home.html
   c. http://www.company/home.html
   d. http://www.company.com/homepage.html

16. HTTP stands for
   a. HyperText Translate Protocol.
   b. HyperText Transfer Pilot.
   c. HyperText Transfer Protocol.
   d. HyperText Transport Pointer.

17. _____ is the second part of a Web site's name and tells you the name of the Web site and the type of institution it is.
   a. Global domain
   b. Domain name
   c. Origin name
   d. URL

18. The global domain .gov means the Web site you are accessing is a
   a. Commercial site.
   b. Government site.
   c. Military site.
   d. Educational site.

19. A link you have previously selected, or followed, appears on the screen in
   a. Red.
   b. Green.
   c. Purple.
   d. Blue.

20. Newest items added to your bookmarks will appear
   a. At the top.
   b. At the bottom.
   c. Alphabetically.
   d. Under the heading, New Entries, at the end of the existing bookmark.

21. To find new or cool pages on the Web, use the
   a. What's New and What's Cool button.
   b. Outstanding button.
   c. Security button.
   d. Latest button.

Skills Review

1. Find, start, and stop links.

a. Start Netscape Navigator.

b. Scroll down and click the <u>Student Online Companion</u> link or <u>Student Offline Companion</u> link on your home page.

c. Find and click the link <u>Exploring business</u> under the heading Explore the Web.

d. Before the page finishes loading, click the Stop button on the Navigation toolbar.

e. Click the Reload button on the Command toolbar to finish loading the page.

2. Move backward and forward.

a. Click the Back button on the Navigation toolbar to return to the Student Online Companion.

b. Click the Forward button on the Navigation toolbar to see the Exploring business page.

c. Continue to select the Back button until it dims.

d. Select the Forward button to display the next page.

e. Choose a link from the page. Once the new page loads, use the Back and Forward buttons to locate the Student Online Companion page.

3. View history.

a. Click the History command on the Windows menu.

b. Double-click WWW Illustrated—Student Online Companion in the list box.

c. Click the Home button.

d. Use the History command to return to the page you just previously viewed.

e. Close the History window.

4. Use bookmarks.

a. Click the Home button.

b. Click the Add Bookmark command on the Bookmark QuickFile menu to add the home page to your list of bookmarks.

c. Load the Student Online Companion or Student Offline Companion.

d. Add the current page to your bookmarks list.

e. Find and select the link <u>Exploring electronic publishing</u> under the heading Explore the Web.

f. Select the Edit Bookmarks command on the Bookmarks QuickFile menu.

g. Use the Bookmarks window to return to the WWW Illustrated—Student Online Companion.

h. Return to the Exploring electronic publishing page and add it to your bookmarks list.

i. If you're working in a lab, remove the bookmarks you added.

5. Work with frames.

a. Select the Home button.

b. Choose the <u>Student Online Companion</u> or <u>Student Offline Companion</u> link.

c. Click the <u>Frame version of this Student Online Companion</u> link.

d. Click the link <u>Exploring the Web</u> in the left frame menu, then select Exploring business.

e. Move back a frame, to display the original content in the right frame.

f. Select another left frame menu link, and move back again using the right-mouse button menu.

g. Click the Home button on the Navigation toolbar to display your home page.

6. Take a guided tour.

a. Select the What's Cool command from the Guide button on the Navigation toolbar.

b. Scroll down the page and click an interesting site to visit.

c. Explore the links, if any, at the site.

d. Click the Home button on the Navigation toolbar.

7. Enter a URL address.

a. Click the Location text box on the Location toolbar.

b. In the Location text box, type "http://www.ibm.com/".

c. Press Enter.

d. Explore this Web site using the techniques and tools you learned about in this unit.

e. Click the Home button when you are done, and exit Netscape Navigator.

▶ Independent Challenges

1. You are the administrative assistant to John Prescott, the president of Words and Wisdom, a small promotional company that specializes in writing ads, promotional pieces, and jingles. John travels a great deal promoting his company's services. He wants to trade in his desktop computer for a laptop he can take with him on his business trips. He has narrowed the search down to five computer makers, and he asks you to investigate their offerings using the Web. These are the computer firms' URLs:

http://www.compaq.com/
http://www.ibm.com/
http://www.apple.com/
http://www.hp.com/
http://www.nec.com/

Use Netscape Navigator to research what information is available on the Web concerning these firms, and print a page from the site of the firm you think offers the most attractive laptop computer line.

2. You recently landed a job as a columnist for a popular computer magazine. One of your responsibilities will be to write a monthly column called Tech Update, which will chronicle the latest developments in hardware technology. Add the following Web sites to your bookmarks so you can browse them for information that will help you stay abreast of what the major players in the technology industry are doing.

http://www.compaq.com/

http://www.ibm.com/

http://www.apple.com/

http://www.hp.com/

Once you store the initial pages of these sites in the bookmarks, use the list to revisit the initial page for each site and investigate the company's offerings. Print a page of the site that most impresses you, and then remove all four sites from the bookmarks.

3. In a few months, you will be graduating from college with a teaching degree. You have been examining the job market and are feeling quite discouraged. A friend suggests you look into the Peace Corps, and you decide to look into the organization and see what it is all about. You remember that AT&T has put its 800-number directories on the Web. Use the following URL to look up the 800 number for the Peace Corps, located in Washington, D.C.

http://att.net/

After you locate the 800-number, print a copy of the page containing the number.

4. Your parents have decided to buy a computer for the family to use. Your parents want to buy a reliable but medium priced (around $2,000) machine. Enter one of the following URLs to investigate the features and prices of a new desktop computer.

http://www.gateway.com/

http://www.dell.com/

http://www.compaq.com/

http://www.ibm.com/

http://www.hp.com/

Print the most interesting page you find with a computer offering the features you like and costing around $2,000.

▶ Visual Workshop

Use the skills you have learned in this lesson to open the Web page shown, and then navigate as necessary to make both the Back and Forward buttons active, as in Figure B-13 below. Print a copy of the page.

FIGURE B-13

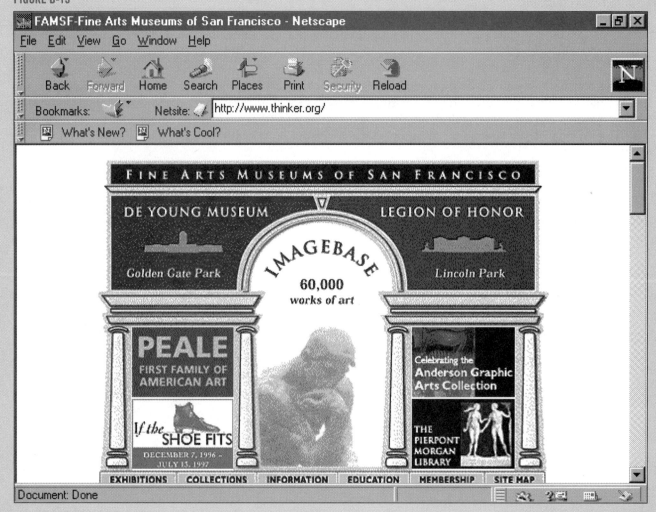

Searching
the Web

Objectives

- ► **Understand search methods**
- ► **Search by subject**
- ► **Search multiple directories by subject**
- ► **Search by guide**
- ► **Search by location**
- ► **Search by content**
- ► **Search multiple indices by content**
- ► **Search by people**

In the last unit, you learned how to navigate the World Wide Web using Netscape Navigator. However, the Web is an enormous network, and simply navigating from one page to the next is a very slow and inefficient way to find information on a specific subject. Fortunately, there are a number of search tools on the Web to help you quickly locate what you want. The major tools include **subject directories** (lists grouped and arranged by topic), **directories of directories** (lists of multiple subject directories), **guides** (pathfinders that suggest new, outstanding, and unusual Web spots), **location maps and directories** (graphics and lists that organize Web sites geographically), **search engines** (searchable indices of the textual content on Web pages), **meta search engines** (single forms for querying multiple indices simultaneously), and **people finders** (indices for locating people).   In this unit, you will learn how to use these search tools effectively and efficiently to locate information for The Nut Tree's online marketing effort.

Understanding Search Methods

Information on the Web is rapidly growing, not well organized, and sometimes inaccurate. As a consequence, it is important to search as effectively and efficiently as possible. Typically, an integrated approach that combines the available search tools gives you the best chance of finding the information you want. Table C-1 indicates strategies for finding information with each of the major search tools. Use the following integrated strategies, or guidelines, to minimize your search time and maximize search results.

 Search broadly, at first, to determine the breadth of information available on the subject.

 Look for pages with collections of links to the subject.

 Find new, outstanding, and unusual Web pages.

 Locate sites related to the subject.

 Search narrowly and deeply to find specific information.

 Navigate the links that sound interesting to locate additional resources on the topic (this activity is often referred to as **surfing the Web**).

 Locate people using "white page" sites.

QuickTip

The Student Online Companion lists many useful search tools. Clicking the Search button on the Command toolbar of Netscape Navigator also provides a list of several popular Web search sites.

Warning about Web information

Information on the Web is typically entered and maintained by volunteers. Thus, this data is not always reliable or well organized. Be skeptical of what you find on the Web, and always attempt to verify its completeness and accuracy with other sources. Also, try to look for reputable sources that are well known (e.g., Harvard Business School).

TABLE C-1: Strategies for searching the Web

to find	example	search by	tools
General categories of information	Overview of electronic publishing on the Web	Subject	Subject directories (e.g., Yahoo! and the WWW Virtual Library)
Wider selection of categories of information	Broader overview of electronic publishing	Subject	Directory of directories (e.g., InterNIC Directory of Directories and Meta Directory of Non-Profit Organizations)
The new, cool, and unusual pages	New company home pages	Guide	Guides (e.g., Web Guide and Web Hotspot)
Regional Web site	Commercial Web sites in Milwaukee, WI	Location	Location maps and directories (e.g., Excite City.Net Region, Online Now)
Narrow and specific information	Web server software	Content	Search engines (e.g., AltaVista, Excite, and HotBot)
Extensive list of narrow and specific information	Web server software	Content	Meta search engines (e.g., WebCrawler, SavvySearch, and Search.com)
A person's e-mail or Web site address	A friend's e-mail address	People	People finders (e.g., Four 11, the Internet White Pages, Switchboard, and World Wide Registry)

Searching by Subject

If you are unsure of where to start investigating a subject or you want a quick overview of the subject, begin your search with a subject directory. A **subject directory** is a list of links to topics arranged alphabetically to facilitate browsing. Experts usually compile subject directories, making them a fairly reliable search tool. These hand-compiled directories also typically list subtopics beneath each major heading, as shown in Figure C-1. This hierarchical organization, or hierarchical tree, lets you quickly browse the available subjects and their subtopics. Melissa Shea, owner of The Nut Tree, asks you to find out more about what commercial services exist on the Web to help establish an online presence for the company. You can use Yahoo! to determine what types of business services are available via the Web.

Steps 1 2 3 4

1. Start Netscape Navigator and click the link for the <u>Student Online Companion</u> on your home page, or, if you are working offline, click the link for the <u>Student Offline Companion</u>.

   The Student Online Companion for this textbook appears in your document window.

2. Scroll down under the heading Search the Web to find and click the <u>Searching by subject</u> link

   A page with links to subject directories displays in your document window.

3. Scroll down to find and click the link <u>Yahoo!</u>

   The Yahoo! home page opens, as shown in Figure C-2. The top of the page features a search form to assist in locating a subject (you will learn about search forms in the lesson "Searching by Content"). For now, you will browse the subject directory, just below the search form, to gain an overview of the business resources available on the Web.

4. Find and click the <u>Business and Economy</u> link in the subject directory

   The list for this category appears, as shown in Figure C-3.

5. Scroll down to find and click the <u>Electronic Commerce</u> link

   A directory of electronic commerce resources displays in your document window.

6. Scroll down the list and examine the available topics

7. When you are done, click the Home button [Home] on the Navigation toolbar

   Your home page reappears in the document window.

Trouble?

If you are unable to connect to Yahoo! (i.e., if you receive an error message or the page fails to load after a long time), select another subject directory from the *Searching by subject* page and explore its structure to complete this lesson.

FIGURE C-1: Alphabetical and hierarchical structure of a subject directory

Major subject heading

Subtopic

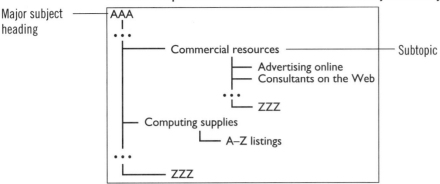

FIGURE C-2: Yahoo! home page

Business and Economy link

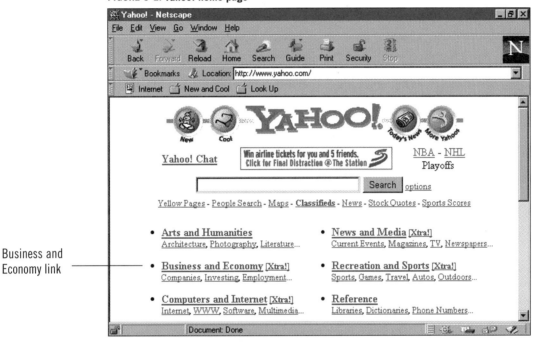

FIGURE C-3: Listing of Business and Economy subtopics on Yahoo!

Electronic Commerce link

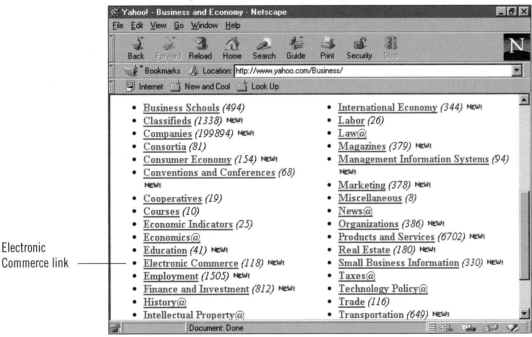

Internet

Searching Multiple Directories by Subject

A **directory of directories**, or a **meta directory**, provides links to many of the subject directories on the Web. A meta directory may point to subject directories that are only related to a particular subject or it might point to a wide variety of subject directories. Typically compiled by a person rather than by automated Web-searching software, a directory of directories often includes useful descriptions of the unique features of each subject directory. This helps you to rapidly identify the most relevant directories to browse. ◢ Melissa wants to make sure the subject-oriented search for Web business resources has been fairly exhaustive. She asks you to use a directory of directories to get the broadest overview possible of subject directories that might help you in your online marketing research.

1. Click the <u>Student Online Companion</u> link or the <u>Student Offline Companion</u> link on your home page, then once it loads, click the <u>Searching multiple directories by subject</u> link

2. Click the link <u>InterNIC Directory of Directories</u>
   The InterNIC Directory of Directories page opens.

Trouble?

If InterNIC is unavailable, browse one of the other listed meta directories.

3. Scroll down and click <u>Browse the Directory of Directories</u>, then scroll down to the Table of Contents and click the <u>Directories</u> link
   The list of subject directories at InterNIC appears, as shown in Figure C-4.

4. Scroll down the Table of Contents, taking time to look at the names of links that might offer business resources, then find and click the link <u>ComFind global business directory and search engine</u>
   A page at InterNIC appears describing the ComFind global business and search engine as the largest global business directory on the Internet.

5. Scroll down the description page and click <u>directory/comfind WWW Server</u>
   After some time, the home page for ComFind loads, as shown in Figure C-5.

6. Click the <u>Category Selection</u> link in the left frame menu
   The ComFind: Find a Category page appears. It offers a search form and A—Z browsing capabilities. Since you are browsing, you'll use the A—Z listings.

7. Click the letter **B** in the A—Z listings. Once the page of subjects starting with the letter "B" appears, scroll down to the topics beginning with the word "Business" at the bottom of the page
   A listing of business resources appears in your document window listed alphabetically, as shown in Figure C-6.

8. Explore one of the business-related links; if you are prompted to choose between global and USA resources, choose the Go! USA Search button. When you are finished exploring, click the **Home button** [Home]

FIGURE C-4: Subject directories at InterNIC

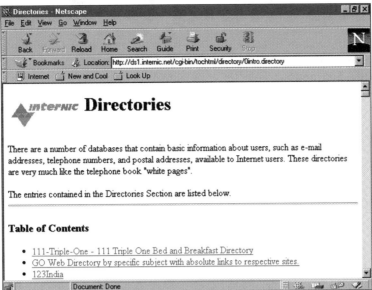

FIGURE C-5: ComFind home page

Menu in frame —

Categories option —

FIGURE C-6: Listing of business resources

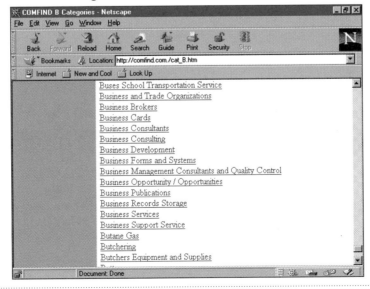

Internet

Searching by Guide

There are hundreds of thousands of Web sites and, even more astonishing, the number of sites continues to double about every two months. To help Web users find the new, outstanding, interesting, and unusual Web sites, individuals and organizations have created Web **guides**, which list the sites they think are among the best of the Web. Some guides provide descriptions and rate the sites for such things as aesthetics, content, and usefulness. ✎ Intrigued by what you have found so far, you decide to use a guide to help you find some of the best commercial resources on the Web.

1. Click the **Student Online Companion** link or the **Student Offline Companion** link on your home page
   The Student Online Companion home page displays.

2. Click the **Searching by guide** link
   A page with links to directory and guide pages appears.

3. Click the **CINET** link
   The Welcome to CNET home page appears, as shown in Figure C-7.

Trouble?

If the links, or image links, in this or subsequent steps have changed, look around for other links or image links to business resources.

4. Scroll down the page and watch the index on the left edge of the page until you find the link **Best of the Web** under the heading REVIEWS, then click the link
   The document window changes to display the Best of the Web page, as shown in Figure C-8.

5. Click the **find sites by category** image link
   The find sites by category page appears.

6. Scroll down the page and click the **business** image link
   A page of alphabetically arranged business links displays, as shown in Figure C-9.

7. Explore some of the business links that interest you

8. When you are finished, click the **Home button** 🏠
   Your home page reappears in the document window.

FIGURE C-7: The Welcome to CINET page

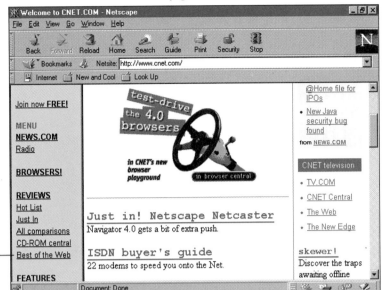

Best of the Web
page link

FIGURE C-8: Best of the Web page at CINET

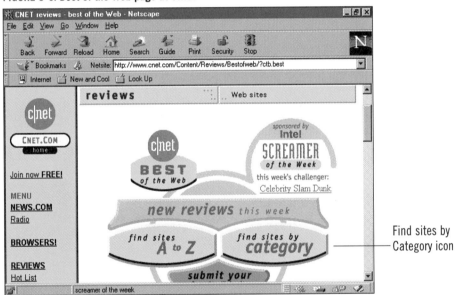

Find sites by
Category icon

FIGURE C-9: Alphabetically arranged business links

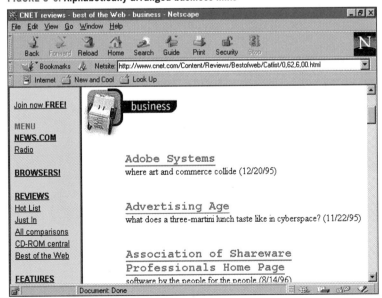

Internet

Searching by Location

When you want to see what Web sites are available in a certain geographical area, maps provide an excellent way to get a bird's-eye view. **Location maps** are special images that depict Web resources by geographical region. Location maps include labeled areas (imagemap links) you can select for closer examination. For example, a typical location-oriented search begins with a map of the world. You start by clicking the region you want to investigate (e.g., North America). A second map displays, showing the countries in the area. After choosing a country (e.g., the United States), you may be presented with additional maps to narrow your search further. Eventually, you will work your way down to a collection of Web sites for the area you are interested in (e.g., Spokane, Washington). You would like to see what kinds of local businesses and services are available on the Web. The Nut Tree is located in Spokane. You can use Web maps to find a collection of sites to call or visit personally.

Steps

1. Click the <u>Student Online Companion</u> link or the <u>Student Offline Companion</u> link on your home page
The Student Online Companion page appears in the document window.

2. Click the <u>Searching by location</u> link
The Search by location page appears.

Trouble?

If you are using the Student Offline Companion, click the <u>OnLine Now</u> link and replace Steps 4-9 with the following instructions: When the OnLine Now search appears, click the list arrow on the right of the Select Your U.S. City list box, scroll down and click "Spokane-WA," then click the Go icon to the right of the list box. Visit some of the Web sites listed, then return to your home page.

3. Select the <u>Excite City.Net Region</u> link
After a time, the City.Net Regions page appears with a map of the world, as shown in Figure C-10.

4. Click the region labeled **North America**
A map of North America appears in your document window.

5. Click the **United States** region
A map of the United States appears, as illustrated in Figure C-11.

6. Click **Washington** state
A page listing several links by topic to resources available in Washington appears. The left edge of the page displays a hierarchical list of regional choices. You can click on any choice in the left frame to jump back one or more geographical levels (e.g., clicking <u>United States</u> would display the U.S. map again).

7. Scroll down the right edge of the page to beneath the heading Destinations, and click the link <u>Cities</u>
An alphabetical list of cities in Washington state appears.

8. Scroll down the page and click <u>Spokane</u>
A directory of topics for Spokane displays, as shown in Figure C-12.

QuickTip

You can also find Web sites by geographical area with directories. If you know the name of the site you want to find, you can use a directory of Web sites organized by location to search for it. For example, W3 Servers offers Web sites arranged under geographical headings. However, this text-based search method doesn't provide the same geographical overview that maps offer.

9. Explore some of the available sites under a topic or two. When you are finished looking around, click the **Home button**

FIGURE C-10: City.Net Regions page appears with a map of the world

North America —

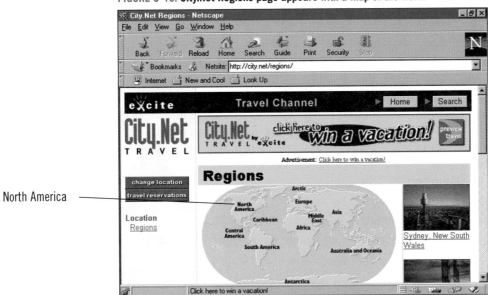

FIGURE C-11: City.Net regional map of the United States

Washington state —

FIGURE C-12: A directory of topics for Spokane

Internet

Searching by Content

When you want to find specific information, your best bet is to use a search engine. A **search engine** lets you specify keywords or phrases to retrieve a list of links to pages on the Web that contain matching information. A search engine uses a special program called a "spider" to travel from one Web site to another, indexing the contents of the Web pages at each site. To search an index, you carefully craft a query using keywords or phrases and enter it in a search form provided by the search engine. A more precisely worded query will yield more relevant results. Impressed by the commercial services you have discovered, you now decide to find a list of agencies that specialize in Web advertising. Since you have a specific topic you want to find, "Web advertising agency," the most expedient way to conduct the search is with a search engine.

Steps

1. Click the <u>Student Online Companion</u> link or the <u>Student Offline Companion</u> link on your home page, then once the Companion page opens, click the <u>Searching by content</u> link
   A page with links to search engines on the Web appears.

2. Click <u>AltaVista</u>
   The simple search form for the AltaVista search engine opens, as shown in Figure C-13. Table C-2 describes the relevant options available in this search form.

QuickTip

In some searches capitalization is important. For example, when searching for proper names like George Washington, correct capitalization is critical to finding what you want.

3. Click the **Search text box** to make the insertion point | appear, and type **"Web advertising agency"**
   The search statement must contain double quotes (") at the end and beginning in the search text box. This tells the AltaVista search engine to only look for documents that contain all your keywords in the precise order in which you have just entered them and together as a phrase. The ability to search for an *exact phrase* really narrows your search results. Without the double quotes, the search engine matches every page indexed that contains any, or all, of the keywords, regardless of where the keywords appear in the documents.

4. Click the **Submit button**
   After some time, the search page reloads with results of the query.

5. Scroll down the page to see the results
   The results appear below the search form, beginning with a summary statement that specifies the number of documents matching your query, as shown in Figure C-14. AltaVista displays the results sorted by how closely they match your query. If a query is poorly constructed, the number of matches, or "hits," can be in the hundreds of thousands, making it nearly impossible to look at all of them.

QuickTip

Search results may also contain other useful hints, like relevancy scores. **Relevancy scores** rate and arrange retrieved Web pages for your optimal viewing. Relevancy scoring typically uses the proximity of keywords (i.e., how close keywords are together) in a document and how often keywords appear in a document to rank the results of a search.

6. Select the first, best matching link
   A page appears in your document window.

7. Examine the document, return to the results page

8. Scroll to the bottom of the page and select the <u>Next</u> link to see the next set of links leading to matching documents

9. Explore one of these links, then click the **Home button** 🏠

Constructing successful queries

If you want your query to a search engine to return the most relevant results, you'll need to construct it using Boolean operators. **Boolean operators** are special connecting words that indicate the relationship among the keywords in your search statement. The Boolean operators **AND, OR,** and **NOT** let you narrow, broaden, or exclude information retrieved in a search, respectively. For more information on using Boolean operators, read the tip or help section on a search engine page.

FIGURE C-13: AltaVista search form

Search drop-down menu

Search text box

Advanced icon

Simple icon

Products icon

Help icon

Display the Results drop-down menu

Submit button

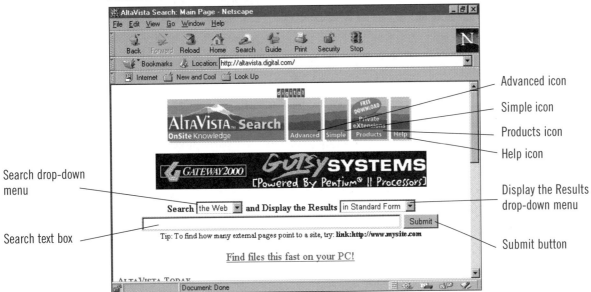

FIGURE C-14: AltaVista search results

Total number of document matches

Number of matches displayed

Links to matching documents

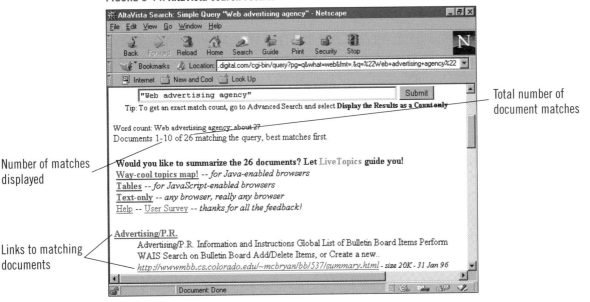

TABLE C-2: Options in the AltaVista search form

option	description
Advanced icon	Switches to a search form with more detailed querying features
Simple icon	Displays the regular (default) search form
Products icon	Offers private extensions for the search engine
Help icon	Provides useful search tips on using the simple and advanced search forms to obtain the most relevant results
Search drop-down menu	Allows selection of Web or USENET newsgroups to search
Display the Results drop-down menu	Specifies whether the search results appear in standard or a compact form
Search text box	Allows entry of search statement
Submit button	Starts the searching process

Internet

Searching Multiple Indices by Content

A **meta search engine** offers a single form to search a variety of powerful search engine indices simultaneously based on keywords or phrases. These unified search interfaces provide a very powerful, convenient, and quick way to cover a lot of ground quickly. However, they also require more Internet resources and should therefore be used judiciously to help make sure that resources are also available to other Internet users. ➤ To ensure that you have a comprehensive collection of Web advertising agencies to assist The Nut Tree in establishing its marketing presence on the Web, Melissa asks you to use a meta search engine to check the major search engine indices simultaneously for other possible agency listings.

Steps 1234

1. Click the <u>Student Online Companion</u> link or the <u>Student Offline Companion</u> link on your home page, then click <u>Searching multiple indices by content</u>

2. Click <u>MetaCrawler</u>

   The search form for MetaCrawler opens, as shown in Figure C-15. Table C-3 describes the relevant options available in this search form.

3. Click the **Search for text box** and type **Web advertising agency**

4. Click the **as a phrase option button**

   This ensures that the search engine indices that are queried only return the documents containing the exact phrase specified in your search statement, allowing you to enter the keywords without quotation marks.

5. Click the **Complete Search button**

   As the querying of each search engine index proceeds, MetaCrawler displays the number of matches returned from each site. When the complete search is completed, MetaCrawler displays a listing of Collated Results with the total number of matches found, as shown in Figure C-16.

6. Scroll down the page to view the results and explore a link or two

7. Click the **Home button** 🏠

Trouble?

You may have noticed that AltaVista returned fewer matches using MetaCrawler than it did when directly queried in an earlier lesson. Individual search engines often offer unique querying configurations and capabilities that are unavailable when using a meta search site. To help you maximize your results, you should use individual search engines in conjunction with meta search engines.

FIGURE C-15: MetaCrawler search form

Search text box

Any option button

All option button

As a phrase option button

Fast search button

Complete search button

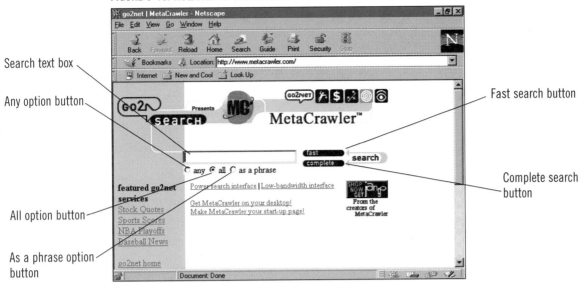

FIGURE C-16: MetaCrawler's collated results from query

Search engine providing this link

Number of matches

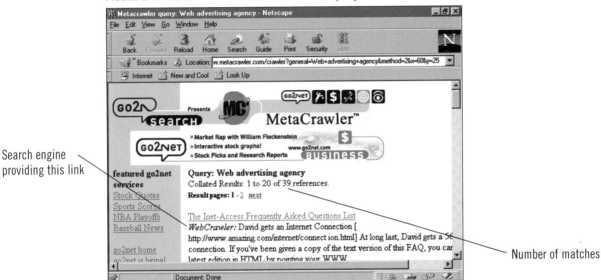

TABLE C-3: Options in the MetaCrawler search form

option	description
Search for text box	Allows entry of keywords or phrases to search for
As a phrase option button	Tells the search engines to return pointers for only the documents that contain the exact phrase specified in the query
All option button	Informs the search engines to return only documents that contain all the words in the query
Any option button	Tells the search engines to return documents that match any of the words in the query
Fast search button	Provides a quick query of search engines
Complete search button	Offers a more extensive query of search engines

Searching by People

A **people list search site** assists you in locating some of the 30 to 60 million people on the Internet. You search for a person's e-mail address, Web page, and other contact information by name and additional variables. Most people directories rely on the individual's name as the key search variable, while others let you specify query topics like company, area, college attended, et cetera. Melissa has lost touch with an old friend who might be of help in setting up The Nut Tree's Web site. She remembers that her friend Kim Nickerson is living on the East Coast, but she is not sure in which state. You can use a people list search site to provide Melissa with a list of people with the same name and their locations.

Steps

1. Click the <u>Student Online Companion</u> link or the <u>Student Offline Companion</u> link on your home page, then click the <u>Searching by people</u> link

A page with links to people finders appears. Note that each tool has unique searching techniques.

2. Scroll down the list and click the <u>Switchboard</u> link

The initial page for the Switchboard appears.

3. Click the **Find people icon**

The Switchboard search form for finding people displays, as shown in Figure C-17. Table C-4 describes the options on this search form.

4. Click in the First Name text box and type **Kim**

The name appears in the text box.

5. Press [Tab], or click in the Last Name text box, then type **Nickerson**

Since you don't know the city or state where Kim lives, leave the City and State text boxes empty.

6. Click the **Search button**

The Security Information dialog box may appear, letting you know that the transmission of data over the Internet will be encrypted to ensure privacy. If it opens, just click the Continue button. After some time, a page appears with the first 8 matches.

7. Scroll down the page, looking for East Coast addresses in the listings. When you reach the bottom of the page, click the <u>More Listings</u> link

8. Repeat step 7 until you reach the end of the listings for Kim Nickerson

9. Exit Netscape Navigator

QuickTip

If you have even a remote idea of the state or city someone might be living in, it's best to enter your guess because it will greatly narrow the results of your search. If the search fails to locate the person, you can always search again using another state or city.

FIGURE C-17: Search form for locating people with Switchboard

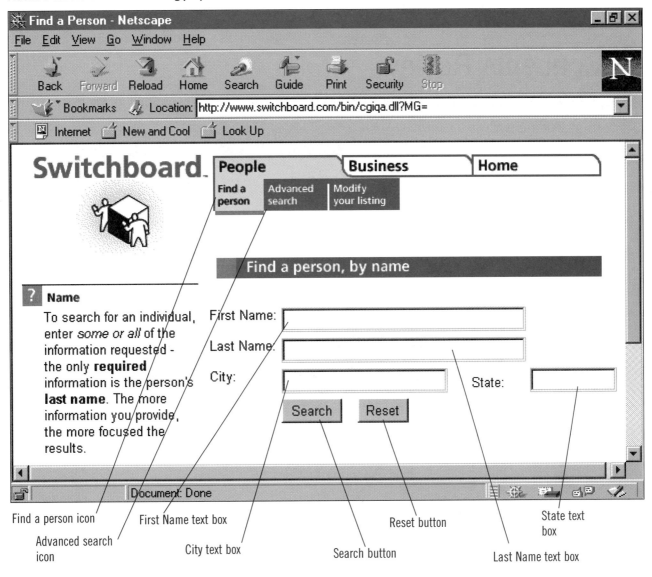

Find a person icon
Advanced search icon
First Name text box
City text box
Reset button
Search button
State text box
Last Name text box

TABLE C-4: Options in the Switchboard search form

option	description
Find a person icon	Displays the simple (default) search form
Advanced search icon	Switches to a search form with more detailed querying features
First Name text box	Allows entry of a person's first name
Last Name text box	Enables entry of a person's last name
City text box	Allows entry of the name of the city where the person lives
State text box	Specifies the state where the person might reside
Search button	Starts the searching process
Reset button	Clears entries in form

Practice

▶ Concepts Review

Briefly describe the four options of the AltaVista search form shown in Figure C-18.

FIGURE C-18

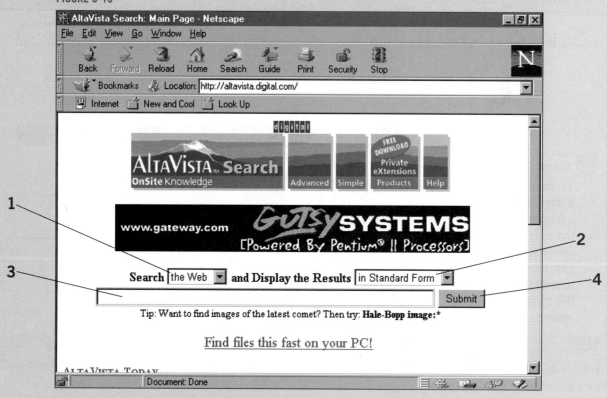

Match each term with the statement that best describes its function.

5. Yahoo!
6. Submit button
7. CINET
8. City.Net Region
9. Switchboard

a. Location-oriented search site
b. Guide site
c. People finder
d. Subject directory
e. Starts the search process

Select the best answer from the list of choices.

10. **Which of the following are NOT search tools?**
    a. Meta search engines
    b. Subject directories
    c. Cards
    d. Guides

11. **Which of the following is NOT a search strategy?**
    a. Search generally at first
    b. Broaden your search using a dictionary
    c. Locate related sites by surfing the Web
    d. Narrow your search with search engines

12. **Yahoo! on the Web is**
    a. A shout of joy.
    b. A location listing.
    c. A content directory.
    d. A subject directory.

13. **CINET is a**
    a. TV series about aliens and government cover-ups.
    b. Guide.
    c. Companion for finding Internet protocols.
    d. Search engine.

14. **AltaVista lets you search by**
    a. Content.
    b. Latitude and longitude.
    c. Manually-compiled subject directories.
    d. Guide.

15. **The City.Net Region lets you search by**
    a. Guide.
    b. Index.
    c. Password.
    d. Location.

16. **The all option button in the MetaCrawler search form lets you**
    a. Tell the search engines to return pointers for documents that match any of the words in the query.
    b. Tell the search engines to return pointers for only the documents that contain the exact phrase specified in the query.
    c. Inform the search engines to return only documents that contain all the words in the query.
    d. Limit the number of capitalized words displayed.

17. **The world map in City.Net Region does NOT display**
    a. Washington.
    b. Asia.
    c. Australia.
    d. North America.

18. **A search engine is a program that lets you query a**
    a. Content index.
    b. Hierarchical subject tree.
    c. List of people.
    d. Index of a meta dictionary.

19. **A directory of directories consists of a**
    a. Page of content indices gathered by a spider.
    b. List of subject directories and often descriptions of the directories' offerings.
    c. List of topics.
    d. People-surfing page.

20. **A meta search engine works by**
    a. Querying a variety of search engine indices simultaneously.
    b. Searching a variety of meta files at the same time.
    c. Querying the best dictionaries on the Web.
    d. Searching for an exact phrase in a URL.

Skills Review

1. Search by subject.

a. Start Netscape Navigator and select either the <u>Student Online Companion</u> link or the <u>Student Offline Companion</u> link on your home page.

b. Select <u>Searching by subject</u>.

c. Choose <u>InfoSpace</u> link.

d. Click the <u>Search by Category</u> link beneath the Yellow Pages icon.

e. Choose the <u>More…</u> link below the Retail icon.

f. Scroll down and click the Gift/Souvenir Shops option button, scroll to the bottom of the page and click the State: list arrow, choose Utah from the State: list box choices, then click the Search button.

g. Examine the top ten listings. To see more listings, click the <u>Next 10 Results</u> link.

h. Return to your home page.

2. Search multiple directories by subject.

a. Select the <u>Student Online Companion</u> link or the <u>Student Offline Companion</u> link on your home page and choose the <u>Searching multiple directories by subject</u> link.

b. Select the <u>Argus Clearinghouse</u> link.

c. Choose <u>Business & Employment</u> from the list of directories.

d. Pick the subcategory <u>marketing</u>.

e. Select <u>Internet marketing or marketing (general)</u> from the Keywords list and explore a guide from the list that appears.

f. Return to your home page.

3. Search by guide.

a. Select the <u>Student Online Companion</u> link or the <u>Student Offline Companion</u> link on your home page, then choose <u>Searching by guide.</u>

b. Select <u>FishNet Web Guide</u>.

c. Scroll vertically and horizontally to check out some of the links to interesting and fun sites on the Web.

d. If you encounter a drop-down list box, simply click the tiny down arrow on the right of the list box to display a menu, select a spot you want to visit, and then select the Go button on the right.

e. Return to your home page.

4. Search by location.

a. Open the Student Online Companion.

b. Choose <u>Searching by location</u>.

c. Select <u>Excite</u> <u>City.Net Region</u>.

d. Select the Asia region.

e. Click on the island of Taiwan.

f. Explore some of the topics about the country.

g. Return to your home page.

5. Search by content.

a. Go to the Student Online Companion or Student Offline Companion.

b. Choose Searching by content.

c. Select HotBot.

d. Click in the search text box to display the insertion point.

e. Type "Free Web consulting" (do not type the quotation marks).

f. Select the tiny down arrow (on the right of the "for" text box) and select the option "the exact phrase."

g. Click the Search icon or press [Enter].

h. When the search results appear, scroll down the list and explore one or more of the links.

i. Try the search again but change the phrase to "consulting." Notice that the broader term "consulting" returns many more document matches.

j. Return to your home page.

6. Search multiple indices by content.

a. Go to the Student Online Companion or Student Offline Companion and choose Searching multiple indices by content.

b. Select Savvy Search.

c. Click in the search text box.

d. Type "Free Web consulting" (do not type the quotation marks).

e. Scroll down the search form and use the drop-down list box to select all "query terms, as a phrase".

f. Click the Integrate results check box so that the results from all the search engines will be displayed in a single report.

g. Scroll back up and click the SavvySearch! button.

h. After some time, the results appear in your document window.

i. Explore one of the more interesting links and the return to your home page.

7. Search by people.

a. Go to the Student Online Companion or Student Offline Companion, click Searching by people, then select Four 11 the Internet White Pages.

b. Type the following name in the appropriate text boxes: "Scott Adams". (*Hint:* If a Security Information box appears, click Continue.)

c. In the Domain text box, type ".com".

d. Select the Search button.

e. After some time, Four 11 returns a list of people, and their e-mail addresses, matching the name you entered.

f. Exit Netscape Navigator.

▶ Independent Challenges

1. As you begin your first week as the columnist for a new magazine dedicated to covering business on the Web, familiarize yourself with the current issues in electronic commerce. From the Student Online Companion or Student Offline Companion home page, choose <u>Searching by subject</u>. Use the subject directory <u>The WWW Virtual Library</u> to find out what commercial services are listed under the <u>Category Subtree</u> link. Explore two of these topics, and write a separate paragraph summarizing each subtopic to bring to the magazine's next issue-planning meeting scheduled for later in the week.

2. A recent article you read mentioned a Web guide called FishNet℠. On the Student Online Companion or Student Offline Companion home page, click <u>Searching by guide</u>, then click the <u>FishNet Web Guide</u> link. Explore some Web sites and print your favorite page for future reference.

3. After speaking with a Peace Corps representative and reviewing the large packet of information they mailed to you, you discover there are several teaching positions open in South Africa for which you would be eligible. However, you know very little about this country. Use the City.Net Region maps to find out about the
1. Size of the country,
2. Climate, and
3. Size and growth rate of the population of South Africa.
(*Hint*: Use the <u>1995 World Factbook: South Africa</u> link)

4. John Prescott, your boss at Words and Wisdom, was very pleased with how well you utilized the World Wide Web to help him make an informed choice for a laptop computer. He now suggests you use the Web to find information that would be helpful in solving some of the company's other computing needs. For example, he is interested in purchasing Web server software. Find some online sources that sell Web server software. You can use a search engine to find "virtual" outlets that sell server software over the Web. Print a copy of the most interesting site you find. Your printout should look similar to the one shown in Figure C-19.

FIGURE C-19

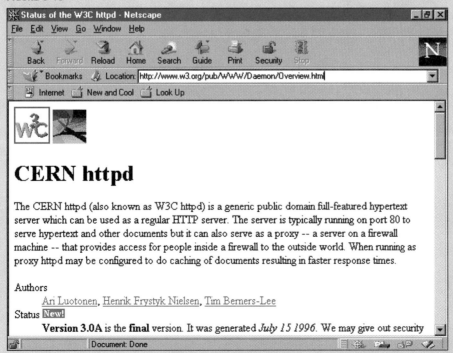

Internet

► # Visual Workshop

Use the skills you learned in this unit to locate a site on the Web that sells nuts, preferably in gift packages, similar to the page shown in Figure C-20. Print a copy of the page.

FIGURE C-20

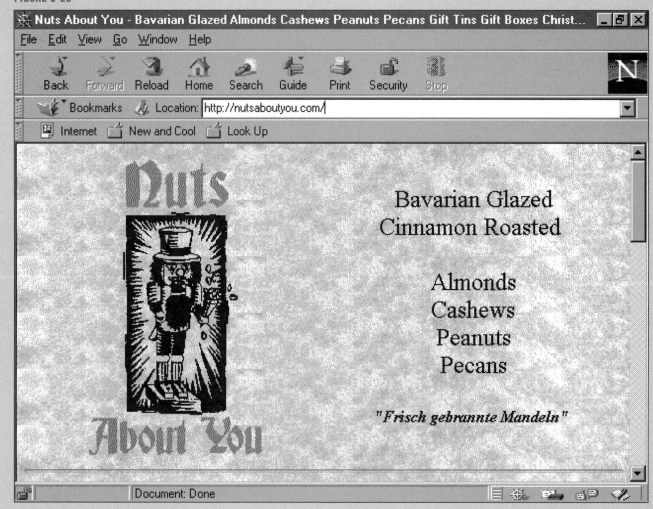

Exploring
the Web

Objectives

▶ **Understand categories of information on the Web**
▶ **Explore business**
▶ **Explore education**
▶ **Explore electronic publishing**
▶ **Explore entertainment**
▶ **Explore government**
▶ **Explore home pages**
▶ **Explore virtual communities**

Now that you know how to navigate and search the World Wide Web, it's time to explore some of the major categories of activity on the Web. In this unit, you'll take a look at the areas of business, education, electronic publishing, entertainment, government, home pages, and virtual communities. You'll visit shopping malls, universities, museums, government sites, personal home pages, and online subculture pages.

✎ As marketing manager for The Nut Tree, you need to know more about the interests and desires of your potential customers so that you can better design a company home page that appeals to Web users. You decide to explore some of the major areas of interest on the Web to see what types of sites and information are attracting Web users. You may find some useful information for your marketing efforts as well.

Understanding Categories of Information on the Web

Understanding how the information on the Web is organized is useful because it makes it easier to locate the information of interest to you. One way to look at the immense traffic on the Web is to divide it into categories, or areas of interest, such as business, education, electronic publishing, entertainment, government, virtual communities, research, science, technology, and so forth. The following bulleted list contains seven of the more popular categories of interest on the Web. The Student Online Companion provides a guide to these areas under the heading "Explore the Web," as shown in Figure D-1. This area list is not intended to be a comprehensive representation of what's on the Web. Instead, the focus is on the types of sites that attract visitors. This "guided tour" will be particularly useful as you determine how to design The Nut Tree home page to attract a high volume of potential customers.

 Business—banks, investing, employment, shopping, and other business resources

 Education—libraries and schools on the Web

 Electronic publishing—electronic books, magazines (e-zines), and newspapers

 Entertainment—art, humor, movies, music, TV, and travel

 Government—U.S. government directories, branches, departments, and independent establishments

 Home pages—personal pages and those of organizations

 Virtual Communities—places where people meet who share similar interests

WWW Illustrated Brief Edition -- Student Online Companion - Netscape

File Edit View Go Window Help

Back Forward Reload Home Search Guide Print Security Stop

Bookmarks Go to: http://www2.coursetools.com/cti/Illustrated/wwwin/

Explore the Web

► Exploring business offers links to variety of commerce-related sites on the Web.

► Exploring education points to libraries and directories of higher education sites on the Web.

► Exploring electronic publishing directs you to electronic books, magazines, and newspapers.

► Exploring entertainment offers art, humor, movies, music, TV, and travel links.

► Exploring government points to U.S. government directories and institutional resource.

► Exploring home pages features a collection of individual and company home pages.

► Exploring virtual communities looks at subcultures of

Document: Done

Web statistics and demographics

Estimates of the number of Internet users run anywhere from 30 to 60 million, with a 10% monthly growth rate. With the exception of e-mail, the Web is by far the most popular service on the Internet. The number of Web sites has surpassed the half-million mark and continues to soar, making available well over 60 million pages of content to Web users. The profiles of those using the Web have also changed profoundly in recent years in terms of age, gender, technical skills, and so forth. For more information and resources on these topics, select the Web statistics and demographics link under the heading About the Web on the Student Online Companion.

Exploring Business

The business area represents the largest and fastest growing domain on the Web. Business-to-business transactions, shopping, investing, employment, and consumer shopping top the list of business areas that interest Web users. Online shopping is rapidly growing in popularity. The Web has an impressive collection of **virtual shopping malls**, which are groups of online store-fronts where companies market their goods and services on the World Wide Web. Just like real malls, virtual malls have their upsides and downsides. For example, a popular virtual mall can greatly increase the number of people who view your home page; however, there will typically be a higher fee for membership in a well-known mall (similar to the fee for leasing space in a real mall). ✎━━━ You decide to visit the Internet Mall, one of the larger and better-known virtual shopping malls, to tour specialty food shops similar to The Nut Tree.

Steps 123 4

QuickTip
You can use some of the links on the Exploring business page under the heading Investing to get free stock quotes. In addition, the heading Other business resources lists valuable links to sites that specialize in helping firms do business on the Web successfully.

1. Start Netscape Navigator and click the __Student Online Companion__ link on your home page, or if you are working offline, click the __Student Offline Companion__ link on your home page, then click __Exploring business__ under the heading Explore the Web
   The Exploring business page appears in your document window. Notice that the top of the page includes a page index. You can click a link in this list to scroll instantly down to the associated topic in the page or you can simply scroll down to the topic with the scroll bar.

2. Select the link __virtual malls__ from the page index (or scroll down to the heading Malls), then click the link __Internet Mall__
   After a brief period, the Internet Mall home page displays, similar to the one shown in Figure D-2. The Internet Mall has over 30,000 stores, ranging from food suppliers to travel agents. The Food and Beverages icon link looks promising for finding specialty snack shops like The Nut Tree.

3. Scroll down the page and click the **Food and Beverage icon**
   The document window changes to display a page like the one shown in Figure D-3. After reviewing the links on the page, the Sweets and Snacks link seems the most likely candidate to lead to shops selling products like yours.

4. Scroll down the page and click the __Sweets and Snacks__ link
   A page listing shops appears.

5. Scroll down the page and select a shop to visit, such as Apples-N-Such
   The store page at the Internet Mall appears. For example, Apples-N-Such's page offers dried Granny Smith and red Delicious apples and dried banana slices, all natural with no preservatives or sulfites added.

6. Explore the page and one or two more shops selling sweets and snacks, then click the **Home button** 🏠
   Your home page reappears in the document window.

FIGURE D-2: Internet Mall

FIGURE D-3: Shopping links to Food and Beverages

Electronic commerce

It's little wonder that retailers are intrigued and concerned about the Internet as a new marketing medium. Forrester Research estimates that Web sales will grow from $518 million dollars to $6.6 billion by the year 2000. Killen & Associates predicts that Web sales could reach $30 billion by the year 2005. At the same time, Goldman Sachs has said that a 10–20 percent switch in the retail market from local store purchasing to virtual sales could eliminate most traditional retailers' profit margins. Thus, the stakes for consumer-oriented businesses couldn't be much higher. For further discussion of this topic and some interesting pointers to other sites dealing with e-commerce issues, select the link Electronic commerce under the heading About the Web on the Student Online Companion.

Internet

Exploring Education

Educational institutions have been active in the Internet community for decades. Not surprisingly, some of the most impressive Web sites are located at colleges and universities around the world. Also, online libraries have recently been attracting quite a bit of attention. This is because libraries on the Web provide publications in an electronic form easily accessible to people around the world. ◆━━ You are considering returning to school to complete a master's degree in business administration to improve your productivity as the marketing manager of The Nut Tree. You can use the Web to explore business programs that might interest you.

Steps

Trouble?

If the Marr/Kirkwood Official Guide to Business School Webs page is unavailable, use another resource on the Exploring education page, under the heading Schools on the Web, to look at graduate business degree programs at schools like Harvard and Stanford.

1. Click the **Student Online Companion** link or the **Student Offline Companion** link on your home page, then click the **Exploring education** link under the heading Explore the Web
   The page listing links to educational resources appears in your document window.

2. Scroll down the page to below the heading Schools on the Web and click **Marr/Kirkwood Official Guide to Business School Webs**
   The home page for the Marr and Kirkwood Official Guide to Business School Webs appears, as shown in Figure D-4. (The term "Webs" is short for a collection of related Web pages that begin with a starting, or home, page.) This guide contains pointers, descriptions, and ratings of business schools.

3. Scroll down and select the link to the **Published B-School Rankings**
   The Published Business School Rankings page opens and displays a variety of ranking schemes.

4. Choose the link **A Side by Side Comparison of 7 Published Rankings of the Best Business Schools**
   A page appears showing the ratings for business schools.

5. Scroll down to the table with the side by side comparison of the rankings by several well-respected publications
   The names of graduate business schools in the United States and internationally are arranged in ascending order (i.e., with the best at the top) by publication, as shown in Figure D-5. Which business schools tend to be in the top ranks?

6. Choose the **Back button** [Back]
   The Published Business School Rankings page reappears. As Online Marketing Manager for Nut Tree, you want information on technology-oriented MBA (Master in Business Administration) programs.

7. Select the **Top 25 Techno MBAs** link
   The top 25 technology-oriented MBA programs, as ranked by the well-known industry trade magazine ComputerWorld, appear.

8. Explore some of the links to the best programs, then click the **Home button** [Home]

FIGURE D-4: Marr/Kirkwood Official Guide to Business School Webs

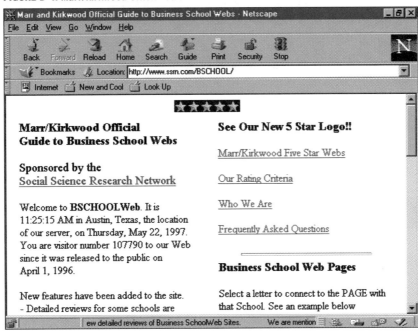

FIGURE D-5: Table listing international graduate business schools

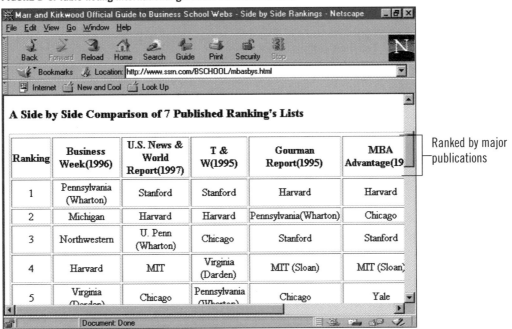

Ranked by major publications

Ranking	Business Week(1996)	U.S. News & World Report(1997)	T & W(1995)	Gourman Report(1995)	MBA Advantage(19
1	Pennsylvania (Wharton)	Stanford	Stanford	Harvard	Harvard
2	Michigan	Harvard	Harvard	Pennsylvania(Wharton)	Chicago
3	Northwestern	U. Penn (Wharton)	Chicago	Stanford	Stanford
4	Harvard	MIT	Virginia (Darden)	MIT (Sloan)	MIT (Sloan)
5	Virginia (Darden)	Chicago	Pennsylvania (Wharton)	Chicago	Yale

Why schools are interested in the Web

The World Wide Web offers a friendly and rich source of information for academic research. It is also a wonderful medium for improving communication between instructors and students. Faculty are finding the Web useful for providing up-to-date course materials such as syllabi and assignments to students, while students are using the Web to create group projects and hypertext papers. There are even entire courses being taught using the Web. The interactive nature of the Web makes it a very useful and attractive means of enhancing classroom instruction. Students really appreciate the ability to control the pace and direction of the learning process.

Internet

Internet

Exploring Electronic Publishing

The number of electronic publishers on the Web is exploding. New electronic books, magazines (e-zines), and newspapers appear almost daily. E-zines are the most popular because they typically use plenty of stunning images (often called "eye-candy"), along with brief but insightful articles (e.g., Hot Wired). Many of these e-zines, or just zines, discuss "lifestyle" issues for those who work and play in cyberspace, while others focus on the technology issues of the Web. You want to investigate an e-zine that covers Web technology to gain a better appreciation of what can be done with The Nut Tree's Web presentation.

1. Use the Student Online Companion or Student Offline Companion to select <u>Exploring electronic publishing</u> under the heading Explore the Web
   A page index appears at the top of the page, with pointers to the topics on the page.

2. Select the <u>Electronic magazines</u> link from the page index, or scroll down to the heading Electronic Magazines (e-zines)
   A list of online magazines appears in your document window.

3. Find and click the <u>Ziff Davis Publishing</u> link, then click the **ZD Magazines button**
   The Ziff-Davis Magazines page looks like the one shown in Figure D-6. The page offers pointers to Ziff Davis's electronic publications. See Table D-1 for a brief description of a few of their online magazines.

4. Click the **PC Magazine** option from the index
   Your document window displays the PC Magazine home page, as shown in Figure D-7.

5. Explore an article or two on this page that looks interesting to you

6. When you complete your explorations, click the **Home button**

Trouble?

If the ZDNET home page has changed and the Ziff-Davis Magazines button is gone, look around the page for another image or set of pointers to the company's online magazines. Remember that the Web is constantly changing, so don't worry if you can't find the ZDNET home page or links to Ziff Davis online publications. Just return to the Exploring electronic publishing page and choose a different link.

TABLE D-1: Sample of Online Ziff-Davis publications

online magazine	description
<u>AnchorDesk</u>	Provides insider analysis of important computer news and top stories.
<u>PC Computing</u>	A guide to products and productivity for today's computing professionals.
<u>PC Magazine</u>	Offers the latest information on the Internet, including daily updates, reviews, and examples of the latest browsers, plug-ins, and Internet development tools.
<u>Computer Shopper</u>	Provides current information on trends in technology, mobile computing, multimedia and a buyer's Guide for both Software and Hardware.
<u>Internet Magazine</u>	Describes the people, products, and strategies behind the latest developments in information technology.
<u>PC Week</u>	Offers comprehensive, up-to-the minute computer industry news, product reviews, and feature articles.

FIGURE D-6: Ziff-Davis Magazines page

FIGURE D-7: PC Magazine Online home page

Links to articles

Internet

Exploring Entertainment

The interactive nature of the Web lets you have all kinds of fun and be entertained. Virtual art collections, galleries, and museums are some of the more eye-catching and inspiring sites to tour on the Web. They feature breathtaking digitized representations of the world's greatest pieces of artwork. In addition, the Web provides an almost endless variety of other entertainment options. There are comics strips and jokes for almost anyone's taste, promotional movie sites stocked with film-related goodies such as downloadable posters and video clips, music hangouts where you can talk about and listen to your favorite bands, and worldwide travel services, to name just a few. After viewing the graphics in electronic magazines in the previous lesson, you are convinced that the inclusion of images in The Nut Tree's Web pages will help entice users to visit the site. However, you are a bit concerned about the loading times of large image files. You definitely do not want to discourage anyone from visiting your site because of irritatingly long delays in displaying your Web page images. To obtain a sense of how long various file sizes can take to load in Netscape Navigator, you decide to take a quick tour of one of the most striking, and sizable, collection of images in the world.

1. Use the Student Online Companion or Student Offline Companion to select <u>Exploring entertainment</u> under the heading Explore the Web

   An index appears at the top of the document window, indicating the available topics on the page.

2. Select the <u>Museums</u> link or manually scroll down to the Museums heading

   A list of links to virtual museums is displayed.

3. Find and click the <u>Web Museum Network</u> link

   The home page for the WebMuseum, Paris, displays in the document window, as shown in Figure D-8. The Web Museum Network is a set of sites around the world that replicate a large collection of famous paintings and other artwork.

4. Scroll down the page to the <u>Famous Paintings</u> link and click it

   The Famous Paintings exhibition page opens.

5. Click the link <u>Artist Index</u>

   An alphabetical list of artists appears.

6. To view a digitized representation of a famous painting, select an artist (e.g., Leonardo da Vinci), explore the painter's page to find a small image of the painting you want to view, then click it

   After some time (especially over a modem), your document window will slowly fill with the much larger view of the painting, like the one shown in Figure D-9. You likely have to scroll up and down (or print the page) to view the entire piece of artwork.

7. When you finish viewing the artwork at the museum, click the **Home button**

FIGURE D-8: **WebMuseum home page**

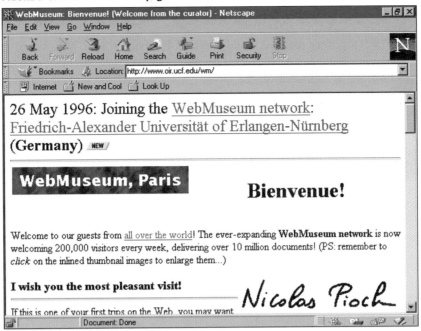

FIGURE D-9: The *Adoration of the Magi* by Leonardo da Vinci

Print the entire painting to see it all at once

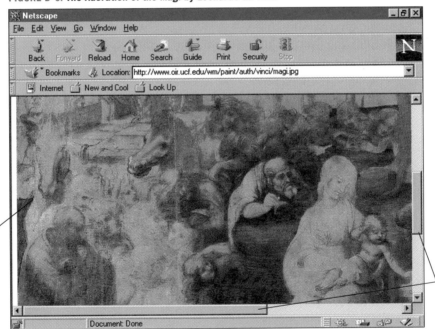

Use scroll bars to view different portions of the painting

Web ethics and law

The question of what responsibilities and rights Web developers have regarding the content they make available on their Web sites is an ongoing debate. This question is both an ethical and legal one. For information on the ethical issues, select the Ethics link under the "About the Web" heading on the Student Online Companion. To find details on the legal concerns, one starting place is the W3 Consortium (World Wide Web Consortium) link under the About the Web heading on the Student Online Companion. Also, a content search using phrases like "Web law in regards to free speech and decency" will help you locate numerous additional resources.

Internet

Internet

Exploring Government

The U.S. government continues to establish services on the Web at such a rate that it is sometimes hard to find the exact site you want. See Table D-2 for a brief description of how the federal government is organized on the Web by branch, department, and independent establishment and government agency. Fortunately, the government does provide a number of subject directory and search engine sites to assist in the location of information within the federal bureaucracy. You want to explore what business help is available from the U.S. government Web sites that represent these institutions. You are especially interested in resources that will help you plan your expansion of The Nut Tree's business into cyberspace.

1. Choose <u>Exploring government</u> beneath the heading Explore the Web on the Student Online Companion or Student Offline Companion
   An index appears at the top of the document window, with links to the major topics on the page.

2. Select the link <u>U.S. Government Directories and Indices</u> or manually scroll down to this heading
   The page scrolls down to display a list of U.S. Web site directories and indices for locating government Web servers and documents. Since you are looking for business assistance, the U.S. Business Advisor seems like a good place to start.

3. Click <u>U.S. Business Advisor</u> under the heading U.S. Government Directories and Indices
   The home page for U.S. Business Advisor opens, as shown in Figure D-10. At this point, you want to gain an overview of what types of resources and online services are available from the government.

4. Click the Browse button at the top of the page
   The Welcome to Browse page opens. This page offers a table with a link, or shortcut, to each main topic on the page.

5. Scroll down to the <u>General Business</u> link either from the table or from the directory further down and click the link
   The General Business page opens, as shown in Figure D-11. An index of the page's topics appears at the top. You are interested in finding out what kind of publications and contacts are available to assist you in your online marketing effort.

6. Scroll down to the <u>Publications/Contacts</u> link in the page index and click it, or scroll down the page manually to the heading <u>Publications and Contacts</u>
   A list of online government publications and contacts is displayed.

7. Find and click the <u>SBA Advocacy Corner [SBA]</u> link from the list
   The SBA Advocacy Corner page appears with a list of links to information discussing important items of concern to small business, as shown in Figure D-12.

8. Explore several of the links, then click the Home button 🏠

Trouble?

If you are unable to connect to the U.S. Business Advisor, select another link on the Exploring government page (e.g., Small Business Administration, Department of Commerce, etc.).

TABLE D-2: Examples of federal resources on the Web

type of federal site	examples
Branch	1. Executive Branch (White House speeches) 2. Legislative Branch (Congressional bills) 3. Judicial
Department (Reports to the Executive Branch)	1. U.S. Department of Commerce (Information on international trade and commerce) 2. U.S. Department of Defense (Military-related information) 3. U.S. Department of Labor (labor statistics)
Independent establishment and government agency	1. Small Business Administration (SBA) (Small business related information) 2. Federal Bureau of Investigation (FBI) (The 10-most-wanted list and other criminal information) 3. U.S. Census Bureau (U.S. census data plus other statistical sources)

FIGURE D-10: U.S. Business Advisor

Browse button displays an alphabetical directory of governmental sites that offer resources for business

FIGURE D-11: General Business page of pointers to government commerce information

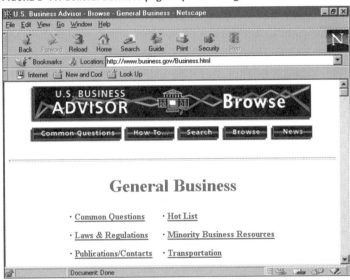

FIGURE D-12: SBA Advocacy Corner page

Links to newsletters, reports, and guides

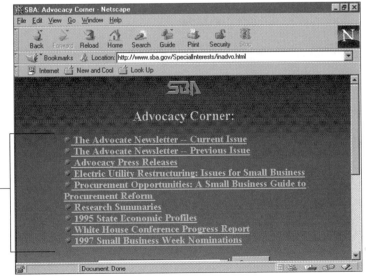

Exploring Home Pages

The Web contains home pages for both individuals and organizations. Personal home pages are typically very innovative and fun to view. They can also be a great source of new ideas for developing unique and attractive company home pages. Although no hard-and-fast rules exist for judging the quality of a home page, Table D-3 describes some general characteristics that are common among the most popular home pages. Keep these characteristics in mind as you view different home pages on the Web. Melissa, now convinced that the Web represents a real business opportunity for The Nut Tree, asks you to design a home page for the company. As a first step, you'll visit a variety of home pages to gather innovative design ideas.

Steps

1. Choose <u>Exploring home pages</u> under the heading Explore the Web on the Student Online Companion or Student Offline Companion
A listing of links to individual and business home pages appears.

2. Click the <u>Personal Pages Worldwide</u> link
The Personal Pages Worldwide University Collections page appears, as shown in Figure D-13. This is a huge directory of universities, arranged alphabetically by school, which lead to student, faculty, and administrator home pages.

3. Scroll down the list and pick a school (e.g., Arizona State University)
A university page appears with information (and possibly listings) of the home pages available at the site.

4. Follow the instructions on the opening page and select a student page (e.g., scroll down the list of home pages and click one, such as Naveed Akbar's Home Page)
The selected home page appears in your document window, like the one shown in Figure D-14.

5. When you finish your explorations, click the Home button 🏠 to return to your home page

TABLE D-3: Characteristics of a good home page

include	don't include
Innovative and eye-catching images	Large images on the home page—bloated images slow loading and, thus, discourage visitors from returning
Unique and valuable information	Long, cluttered, or wordy pages
Short and to-the-point Web pages	Nonfunctioning or outdated links
Links to other related pages on the Web	Links to large files without labels or warnings about their size—users don't want to wait long periods to navigate your site
Warnings advising viewers of the size of files (e.g., still images, sound files, and video clips)	Obscure or hard-to-read icons
Meaningful buttons and icons to help users quickly and easily find what they are looking for	Scattered or random assortment of confusing buttons or impossible to comprehend icons.

FIGURE D-13: **Personal Pages Worldwide University Collections**

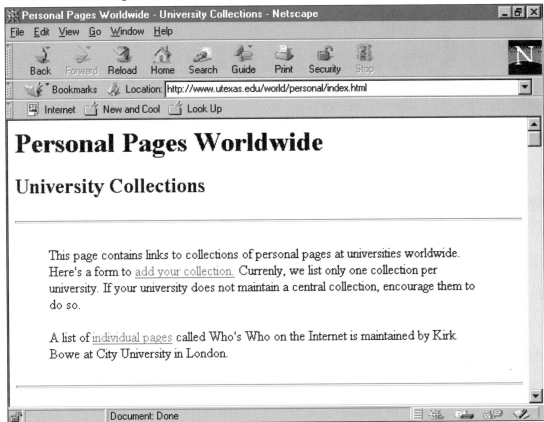

FIGURE D-14: **Sample personal home page**

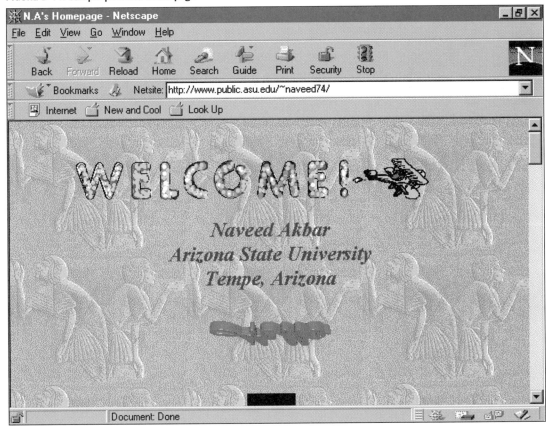

Internet

Exploring Virtual Communities

A **virtual community** is a site in cyberspace where people gather to discuss topics of mutual interest, make friends, and form groups that will help each other through the good and bad times. Like any healthy community, a good virtual community helps heal members with support and advice. A virtual community can also lessen the isolation of cyberspace by providing meeting places where fellow cybernauts share their experiences on the cutting edge of the information age.

Melissa asks you to explore a virtual community to see what support and resources might be available for her and you to better understand this new medium of communications.

Steps 1 2 3 4

Trouble?

Some virtual communities require you to become a member before you are allowed to access their resources and activities. Some sites require membership fees, while others are so well supported by advertising and corporate sponsorships that they can afford to offer free registration.

1. Choose <u>Exploring virtual communities</u> under the heading Explore the Web on the Student Online Companion or Student Offline Companion
   A list of pointers to virtual communities appears.

2. Click <u>GeoCities</u>
   The initial page for GeoCities opens, as shown in Figure D-15. Virtual communities, like GeoCities, often offer home pages, e-mail accounts, and discussion, or chat, forums for their members. GeoCites has over thirty "neighborhoods," or themes, where people of like interests publish Web pages and chat about particular topics.

3. Select the <u>Neighborhoods</u> icon on the top of the GeoCities page
   A page listing topics ranging from the arts to outdoor recreation appears.

4. Scroll down and click <u>ResearchTriangle</u>
   A neighborhood page appears, with a menu frame on the right, as shown in Figure D-16. This theme page is where high-tech visionaries, futurists, and cybercitizens gather to talk about the future of information technology and computing.

5. Explore the options on the page; when you finish go back to the Exploring virtual communities page and choose another site to visit
   The home page for the virtual community appears, like the one shown in Figure D-17.

6. When you are done investigating the site offerings, exit Netscape Navigator

FIGURE D-15: Initial page for GeoCities

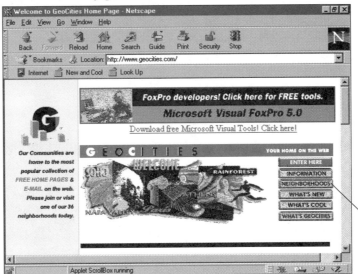

Neighborhoods icon

FIGURE D-16: Research Triangle neighborhood, or theme, page

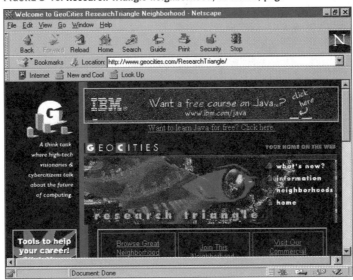

FIGURE D-17: Sample virtual community home page

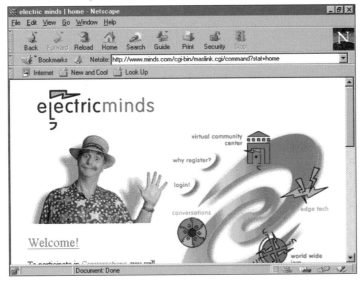

Practice

► Concepts Review

Label the characteristics of a good personal home page indicated in Figure D-18.

FIGURE D-18

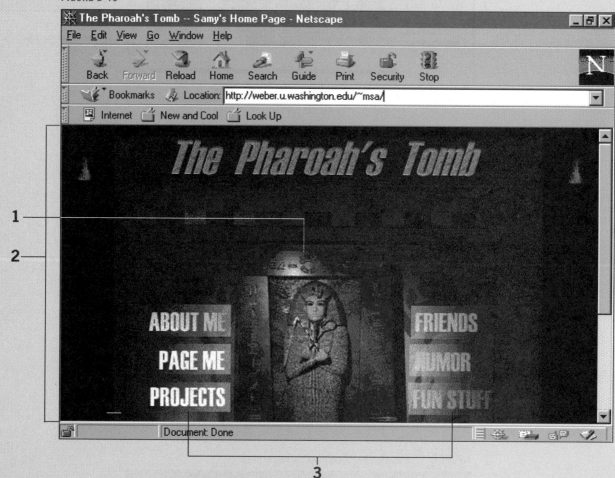

Match each of the terms below with the statement that best describes its function.

4. Virtual storefront
5. PC Magazine on the Web
6. CIA
7. Virtual shopping mall
8. Harvard University

a. Electronic magazine
b. U.S. federal agency
c. School on the Web
d. A place to shop online
e. Online collection of places to shop

Select the best answer from the list of choices.

9. **Which one of the following is NOT a business resource on the Web?**
   a. Banks
   b. Investment sources
   c. Myst
   d. Virtual shopping malls

10. **Which one of the following is NOT an entertainment area of interest on the Web?**
    a. Art galleries
    b. Movies
    c. TV
    d. Interactive moon walks

11. **A virtual shopping mall provides all of the following except**
    a. Online advertising.
    b. A collection of company home pages.
    c. Online purchasing.
    d. A place to meet other people.

12. **The following are all areas of interest for electronic publishing on the Web except**
    a. Electronic books.
    b. Electronic newspapers.
    c. E-zines.
    d. Electronic posters.

13. **Which of the following is NOT a federal government category?**
    a. Department
    b. Office
    c. Branch
    d. Not for profit

14. **Which of the following is NOT a characteristic of a good home page?**
    a. Short and concise
    b. Large, impressive graphics
    c. Links to related resources
    d. Innovative and eye-catching images

15. **The growth rate of the number of Web users is**
    a. 5% per month.
    b. 10% per month.
    c. 5% per year.
    d. 10% per year.

16. Which of the following is NOT a reason why a Web page may take a long time to load?

   a. A large graphical image appears on the page

   b. High traffic on the Internet

   c. The speed of your connection to the Internet

   d. The length of your monitor's AC cord

17. U.S. Business Advisor is

   a. A searchable subject directory and index with links to government business resources.

   b. A commercial computer game.

   c. The Web site for the Budget Office.

   d. A government-produced e-zine on the state of the economy.

18. Which category would you select if you want to find a listing of electronic books?

   a. Home pages

   b. Electronic publishing

   c. Business

   d. Government

19. Which area would you select if you were planning a trip to Europe, and you wanted to find out the best time of year to visit Switzerland?

   a. Entertainment

   b. Education

   c. Business

   d. Government

20. What is the subject of many of today's most popular e-zines?

   a. Cyberspace lifestyle

   b. Commercial

   c. Construction

   d. Health

21. A virtual community is a

   a. 1960's commune style of living.

   b. Group of people who share common interests, become friends, and help each other heal.

   c. Cult of people who refuse to use technology.

   d. Collection of people who roam the Web like nomads of old roamed the desert.

Skills Review

1. Explore business.

a. Start Netscape Navigator.

b. Select the <u>Student Online Companion</u> or <u>Student Offline Companion</u> link on your home page.

c. Choose the link <u>Exploring business</u>.

d. Select the <u>Security Apl Quote Service</u> link under the Investing heading.

e. When the Security Apl Quote Server page appears, scroll down to the Ticker Symbols text box and click it.

f. To get stock quote information on the International Business Machines (IBM) Corporation, type "IBM" and click the Get Quotes button.

g. Review the search results.

h. Use the search form on this page to retrieve a stock quote for MSFT (Microsoft Corporation).
Note: If you get a Security Information dialog box, click Continue.

i. Return to your home page.

2. Explore education.

a. Select the <u>Student Online Companion</u> or <u>Student Offline Companion</u> link on your home page.

b. Click the link <u>Exploring education</u>.

c. Choose the <u>Library of Congress World Wide Web</u> link under the heading Libraries on the Web.

d. Click the <u>American Memory Page</u> link, then select a topic from this page (e.g., Portraits of the Presidents and First Ladies).

e. Explore one of the offerings on the topic you choose.

f. Return to your home page.

3. Explore electronic publishing.

a. Select the <u>Student Online Companion</u> or <u>Student Offline Companion</u> link on your home page.

b. Click the link <u>Exploring electronic publishing</u>.

c. Choose the <u>Mercury Center Web</u> link under the heading <u>Electronic Newspapers</u>.

d. Find and read a news article on the Mercury Center Web page that interests you.

e. Return to your home page.

4. Explore entertainment.

a. Select the <u>Student Online Companion</u> or <u>Student Offline Companion</u> link on your home page.

b. Click the link <u>Exploring entertainment</u>.

c. Choose a link under the heading TV.

d. Investigate what is available at the site.

e. If links to related sites exist (e.g., Other Resources), then explore one of them too.

f. Return to your home page.

5. Explore government.

a. Select the <u>Student Online Companion</u> or <u>Student Offline Companion</u> link on your home page.

b. Click the link <u>Exploring government</u>.

c. Choose one of the links under the heading <u>Independent Establishments</u> (e.g., U.S. Census Bureau).

d. If available, find and read more information about the site (e.g., About the Census Bureau).

e. Examine what the site has to offer.

f. Return to your home page.

6. Explore home pages.

a. Select the <u>Student Online Companion</u> or <u>Student Offline Companion</u> link and then <u>Exploring home pages</u>.

b. Choose a link to personal home pages (e.g., <u>Student, Faculty, and Staff</u> at the University of Kansas).

c. Explore the pages listed at the chosen site for unique and creative designs.

d. Return to your home page.

7. Explore virtual communities.

a. Select the <u>Student Online Companion</u> or <u>Student Offline Companion</u> link and then <u>Exploring virtual communities</u>.

b. Pick a virtual community link (e.g., The WELL).

c. Examine the topics of conversations and types of activities available at this site.

d. Exit Netscape Navigator.

▶ Independent Challenges

1. The computer needs of a rapidly growing PR firm, Words and Wisdom, are becoming expensive. John Prescott realizes he will need to obtain additional funding to purchase state-of-the-art computers and peripherals for his new staff members. He asks you to find out about the business banking services available on the Web. To do this, you'll need to:

1. Select the <u>Student Online Companion</u> link on your home page.

2. Click the link <u>Exploring business</u>.

3. Choose a link under the heading Banks on the Web.

4. Find and read information about the online business-oriented banking services available from this institution.

2. Your American history professor has assigned research topics for the final paper. Your paper is to be on the history of the White House. To gather more information about the Executive Branch of the federal government, do the following:

1. Select the <u>Student Online Companion</u> or <u>Student Offline Companion</u> link on your home page.
2. Click the link <u>Exploring government</u>.
3. Choose the link <u>The White House</u> under the Executive Branch heading.
4. Choose <u>White House History and Tours</u> and explore.
5. Print a copy of the White House's home page to pass in with your research paper.

3. You have applied and been accepted into the Peace Corps, and your first tour to South Africa begins next month. You need to get your financial affairs in order before you leave the country. Explore one of the money management and investment sites listed in the Student Online Companion or Student Offline Companion (e.g., Fidelity Investments Information Center). Determine what resources are available to help you manage your money. Print a copy of the investment site's home page for future reference.

4. An instructor wants to teach her students how to create their own home pages, and she is in search of an example of a page that has a good balance of text and clean graphics. Use the <u>Exploring home pages</u> link listed in the Student Online Companion or Student Offline Companion to find and print two Web pages: a well-designed page and a page that could use some work. Make a list of how the second page could be improved upon. (Be sure to use the characteristics listed in Table D-3.)

Internet

▶ Visual Workshop

Use the skills you learned in this unit to find and print the digitized painting shown in Figure D-19.

FIGURE D-19

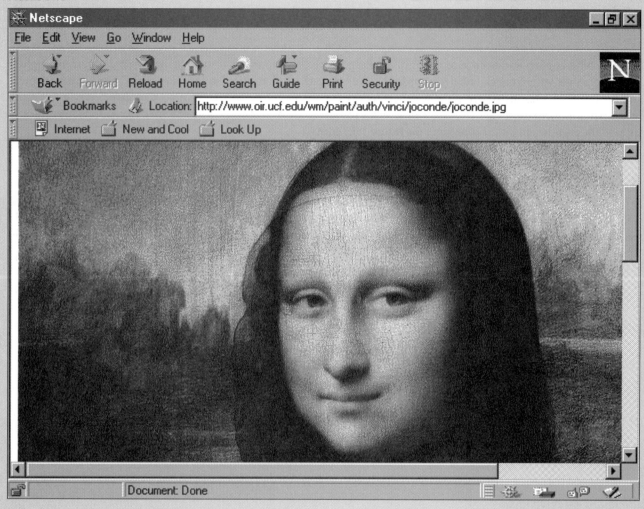

Appendix

Webcasting

with Netcaster

Objectives

► **Find a channel**
► **Subscribe to a channel**
► **Display a channel**

Netscape Netcaster is an integral part of Netscape Navigator 4 that lets you receive personalized information without having to search manually through the growing number of pages on the Web. Much like a TV remote control, Netcaster makes it easy to subscribe, or select, the "channels" of content you want to view. A **channel** is a Web site designed to deliver focused, dynamic, and up-to-date information in an eye-catching multimedia format. Once you subscribe to a channel (e.g., ABCNEWS.com or CNNfn), content is **broadcast**, or delivered directly to your desktop at predefined intervals. A channel can appear as a regular Web page in Netscape Navigator or as a full-screen "webtop." A **webtop** is essentially a borderless Web page that takes over your entire computer screen. Although a webtop replaces your normal desktop with a channel, you can easily turn off the current webtop with an onscreen control and return to your desktop. You can also run webtops in the background and still work on other tasks while the webtops are automatically updated. This lets you keep up with the latest information without sacrificing the use of your computer. In addition to channels, Netcaster can download pages from a standard Web site so you can view them when you're offline (disconnected from the Internet).

Finding a Channel

Netscape Netcaster offers a number of ways to find channels. When you launch Netcaster, the **Netcaster window** appears on the right side of your desktop, as shown in Figure A-1. For a description of the buttons and controls in the Netcaster window, see Table A-1. The Netcaster window looks very much like a TV remote control, displaying a ready-made list of premier channels in the **Channel Finder**. Netcaster also lets you collect a personal list of channels with **My Channels** to make finding your favorite channels even easier. The instructions below offer a basic introduction to finding channels on the Internet with Netscape Netcaster.

QuickTip

To hide the Netcaster window, click the tab (or toggle) protruding out on the left side of the window. To show the Netcaster window, click the tab on the right side of your desktop.

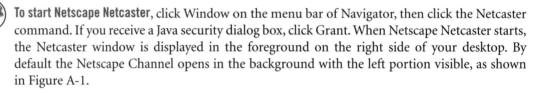

To start Netscape Netcaster, click Window on the menu bar of Navigator, then click the Netcaster command. If you receive a Java security dialog box, click Grant. When Netscape Netcaster starts, the Netcaster window is displayed in the foreground on the right side of your desktop. By default the Netscape Channel opens in the background with the left portion visible, as shown in Figure A-1.

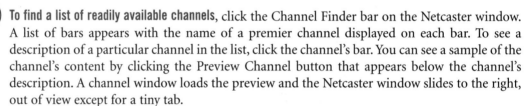

To find a list of readily available channels, click the Channel Finder bar on the Netcaster window. A list of bars appears with the name of a premier channel displayed on each bar. To see a description of a particular channel in the list, click the channel's bar. You can see a sample of the channel's content by clicking the Preview Channel button that appears below the channel's description. A channel window loads the preview and the Netcaster window slides to the right, out of view except for a tiny tab.

QuickTip

Use the triangle-shaped icons on the Channel Finder to scroll up and down the listing of bars.

To find additional channels, click the More Channels bar at the bottom of the list in Channel Finder. A Channel Finder window opens to the left and displays a collection of additional channel listings from the Netscape Web site. You can use options in this window to preview and subscribe to more Netcaster channels.

To find your personal collection of channels, click the bar labeled My Channels in the Netcaster window. The list of the channels you currently subscribe to appears. Like Channel Finder, you can see additional information about a channel by clicking its bar in the list.

To close Netcaster, click the Exit button on the right hand side, near the bottom of the Netcaster window. If you have webtops open, clicking the Exit button also closes them.

FIGURE A-1: The Netscape Netcaster window and Netscape Channel window

Netscape Channel window

Click here to show or hide the Netcaster window

Netcaster window

Channel finder

Buttons

Control icons

TABLE A-1: A description of the options in the Netcaster window

option	description
New button	Opens the Channel Properties dialog with options to add a channel or Web site to the My Channels list
Options button	Opens the Options dialog box with panels to control channel properties, updates, subscriptions, deletions, desktop layout, and security
Help button	Displays the NetHelp window with information on how to use Netcaster
Exit button	Closes Netcaster
	Displays security information about the webtop
	Displays previous page on webtop
	Displays next page on webtop
	Prints the current webtop
	Shows or hides the webtop
	Moves the webtop to the foreground or background
	Closes the webtop
	Opens a Netscape Navigator window
	Shows or hides Netcaster on your desktop

Internet

Subscribing to a Channel

To provide the widest variety possible of Netcaster channels, you can either use the ready-made list from the Channel Finder or click the New button on the Netcaster window to subscribe to any channel manually. Follow the instructions below to add a channel to your personal subscription list in My Channels.

QuickTip

To unsubscribe from a channel or webtop from My Channels, click Options. Select the channel or webtop you want to delete in the Options dialog box, click Delete, then click OK.

To subscribe to a channel with Channel Finder, start Netcaster. A list of channels appears in the window. Click the bar of the channel to which you want to subscribe. Click the Add Channel button below the channel's bar. The Netcaster window slides to the right, out of sight, and the channel's registration information appears in the Channel window. Fill out all the information requested, then click the Continue button in the lower left corner of the Channel window to move through the registration screens (click the Cancel button next to the Continue button at any time to halt the subscription process). Once the channel registration procedure is completed, the channel is automatically included in your My Channels subscription list.

QuickTip

Some channels automatically register as webtops. You can change a webtop back to a channel display by right-clicking on it in My Channels, selecting the Properties command, and specifying that it appear in a Navigator window in the Display pane of the Channel Properties dialog box.

To subscribe to a channel manually, click the New button at the bottom of the Netcaster window. The Channel Properties dialog box appears with options for subscribing to the site, as shown in Figure A-2. See Table A-2 for a brief description of these options. You can use the options in this dialog box to specify a channel subscription and customize it to suit your own tastes (e.g., adjust a channel's update intervals or determine whether the channel displays in a Navigator window or as a webtop). Click OK to save the settings, close the dialog box, then add the channel to My Channels.

FIGURE A-2: **Channel Properties dialog box**

Name text box for channel or Web site —

Location text box for channel —

Update check box —

Drop-down list box specifies delivery intervals —

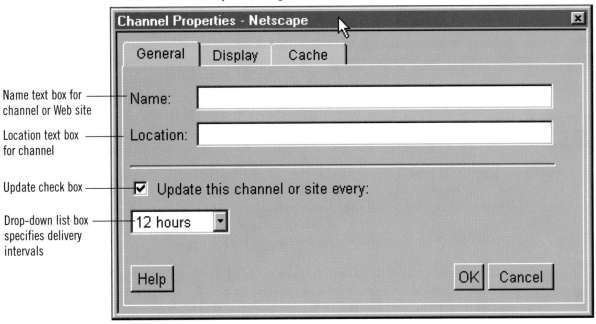

TABLE A-2: **A description of the options in the Netcaster window**

options	description
General Pane	• *Name text box* allows entry of a name for the channel or site • *Location text box* allows entry of the location (URL) • *Update this channel or site every: check box* turns on the automatic channel updating feature • *Update schedule list box* displays a list of options to determine how often the channel is updated • *OK button* closes the Channel Properties dialog box and saves any new settings • *Cancel button* closes the Channel Properties dialog box and does not save changes to the settings
Display plane	• *Default Window option button* specifies that the channel be displayed in a Navigator window • *Webtop Window option button* causes the channel to display as a Webtop
Cache Pane	• *Download text box* determines how many levels deep in the site are automatically updated (i.e., how many series of links are followed) • *Stop Update button* terminates the updating process • *Don't store more than text box* restricts the number of kilobytes (k) of information that can be stored on your local hard disk • *OK button* closes the Channel Properties dialog box and saves any new settings • *Cancel button* closes the Channel Properties dialog box and does not save changes to the settings

Displaying a Channel

Netscape Netcaster channels can be displayed in a number of ways. You can elect to view them in a standard Navigator window or as a webtop anchored to your desktop. In webtop mode, a channel remains a part of your desktop even while other applications are open. A webtop simply remains in the background until you select it to view. The following instructions provide a brief guide on how to control the way Netcaster channels and webtop are displayed.

   To display a channel, open Netcaster, then click a bar from the list in My Channels on the Netcaster window. The channel appears in a Navigator window, as shown in Figure A-3. (Depending on the channel site, the contents may appear in a separate Channel window.) You can close a channel by selecting the Close command from the File menu in Navigator (or clicking the Close button on a Netscape Channel window).

QuickTip

You can make a channel a webtop by right-clicking on the channel's bar in My Channels, selecting the Properties command, and specifying that it appears in a webtop in the Display pane of the Channel Properties dialog box.

To display a webtop, open Netcaster, then select one of the rectangular bars from the list in My Channels. If you already have a webtop open, the current webtop is replaced with the one you just selected. When you open a webtop, it automatically becomes the backmost window on your desktop. Thus, it is initially invisible unless the webtop is the only window open on your desktop. To bring the webtop into the foreground for viewing, as pictured in Figure A-3, toggle open the Netcaster window and click either the Desktop/Webtop button or the Front/Back button .

To hide a webtop, click in the Netcaster window. The desktop appears, and the N logo and webtop controls remain visible. To display the webtop again, select once more.

 QuickTip

Use the Options dialog box to customize other features of Netcaster.

To specify the default channel that opens when Netcaster starts, click the Options button in the Netcaster window, then click the Layout tab in the Options dialog box. The Options dialog box appears, as shown in Figure A-4. Select the Set default to: drop-down list box, then click the channel you want to open when Netcaster starts. If you don't want a channel to open at launch, select the None option button. Click Close to save the new default setting, then close the dialog box. See Table A-3 for a brief description of the features in the Options dialog box.

TABLE A-3: Description of the features in the Options dialog box

section	description
Channels Pane	• *Subscription list box* displays channels in your personal collection in My Channels and lets a channel be selected
	• *Properties button* displays the attributes of the selected channel in the Subscription list box
	• *Update Now button* causes the currently selected channel in the Subscription list box to be updated
	• *Add button* subscribes you to a channel
	• *Delete button* removes the selected channel from the My Channels collection
Layout Pane	• *Attach Netcaster drawer to list box* specifies where the Netcaster window appears on your desktop
	• *Attach Webtop to list box* specifies where the webtop window appears on your desktop
	• *Automatically hide Netcaster window* check box collapses the Netcaster window when a channel or webtop is displayed
	• *None option button* tells Netcaster not to display a default channel when Netcaster first starts
	• *Set default to: option button* allows you to specify a channel to display when Netcaster is first launched
	• *Set default to list box* sets a channel to display when Netcaster is first launched
Security Pane	• *Accept Castnet cookies* check box allows the downloading and storing of a file with information about you on your hard disk which is called a cookie. By default, this option is turned off for your protection (see HelpNet for details).
	• *Enable Castnet logging* check box records a log file with information about Castnet channelcasting
	• *Enable Castnet profiling* check box allows your preferences to be "profiled"

FIGURE A-3: A webtop displayed in the foreground

FIGURE A-4: Options dialog box displaying the Layout pane

None option button
causes no default
channel to display
when Netcaster
starts

Set default to:
drop-down list box

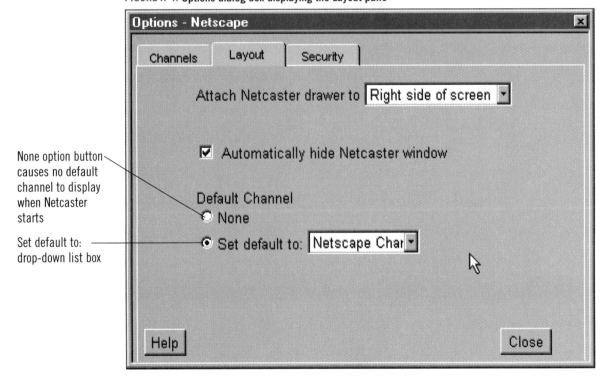

Internet

Glossary

Internet

Address The unique string of text that identifies the location of a Web page on the World Wide Web. *See also* Uniform Resource Locator (URL).

Bookmark The name and address of a Web page (or site) stored in the Bookmarks list.

Bookmark list A feature of Netscape Navigator that enables the user to collect and organize the names and addresses of favorite Web pages (or sites) for quick and easy access in the future.

Boolean operators Special connecting words (i.e., AND, OR, and NOT) that indicate the relationship among keywords in a Web search statement.

Button Causes an action to occur when it is clicked in a form. The user can assign any action to a button.

Calendar *See* Netscape Calendar.

Channel Personalized content that can be automatically delivered, at periodic intervals, to a user's desktop by Netscape Webcasting, or Push, technology.

Channel Finder Like a TV remote control, a list of bars displays a ready-made collection of premier channels as bars.

Collabra *See* Netscape Collabra.

Composer An editor for creating Web pages that provides easy-to-use features to modify, format, enhance, and publish Web presentations.

Conference *See* Netscape Conference.

Content-oriented search A search method that is most effective when searching for information on a specific topic. Requires a search engine. *See also* search engine.

Cursor A blinking vertical line in the document window of an editor that indicates where any new text will appear. Also known as the insertion point.

Discussion group A collection of Internet users meeting electronically to discuss a particular topic of interest by posting and exchanging messages. Also known as a newsgroup.

Document window Displays the current Web page. *See also* Web page, Web document.

Domain name A set of words or letters assigned to represent a particular Web site. For example, www.microsoft.com is the domain name for the Microsoft Corporation and when entered in Navigator's Location text box will cause the browser to display the corporation's home page. *See also* Uniform Resource Locator (URL), Web site.

Electronic mail (e-mail) A system used to send and receive messages electronically.

Electronic publishers Organizations that provide hypertext books, magazines, and newspapers online.

Extranet Refers to business-to-business communication using the Internet.

E-zine The Internet abbreviation for an electronic magazine.

File Transfer Protocol (FTP) A communication standard that allows users to retrieve and send files over the Internet.

Frames A feature of Netscape Navigator that allows users to divide the document window into numerous smaller windows, each containing unique information.

Global domain The last letters of a domain name that indicate the category to which a Web site belongs. For example, the global name extension .edu indicates that the Web site is part of the educational domain on the Internet. *See also* top level domain.

Graphic Illustrates complicated information easily on a Web page. *See also* image.

Groupware Software that enables electronic collaboration between users.

Guide A navigational aid that lists and describes new, unusual, and outstanding Web pages. Also referred to as a tour guide or travel guide.

Guide-oriented search A search method used when trying to locate something new or unusual on the Web. *See also* guide.

Home page The initial Web page that Netscape Navigator loads each time you launch the program. The term is also used to refer to the main page of a Web site. *See also* Web page.

Horizontal scroll bar A screen element that allows users to quickly move left and right through a Web page.

HTML *See* HyperText Markup Language.

HTML source files Simple text files that include HTML tags and can be opened, viewed, and edited with any word processor. *See also* HyperText Markup Language (HTML).

HTTP HyperText Transfer Protocol, the communication standard or protocol established for exchanging information and pages over the Internet. *See also* Uniform Resource Locator (URL), HyperText Transfer Protocol (HTTP).

Hyperregions Graphical links in a Web page that, when clicked, connect users to a group of related Web pages.

Hypertext links Enable the user to open related Web pages by clicking them with the mouse. *See also* strand.

HyperText Markup Language (HTML) The programming language used to describe the general structure of a Web page. HTML uses special character strings, called tags, to enable browsers to properly display the contents of a Web page. *See also* tags, structuring tags, formatting tags.

HyperText Transfer Protocol (HTTP) The communication standard established for the World Wide Web that ensures that every computer accessing the World Wide Web is using the same language when sending and receiving Web pages.

Icon A symbol used to represent a command.

Image A graphical illustration (e.g., picture, drawing, or painting) displayed on a Web page.

Image tag An HTML tag used to insert a graphic in a Web page. *See also* HyperText Markup Language (HTML), tags.

Internet A collection of networks that connect computers all over the world together using phone lines, coaxial cables, fiber optic cables, satellites, and other telecommunications media. *See also* network.

Internet e-mail address Used to send someone mail electronically, it consists of the recipient's user name, the @ symbol, and the domain name of the host (mail server).

Internet Protocol address The direct, or actual, address of a computer on the Internet. An IP (Internet Protocol) address consists of a series of numbers, separated by dots (e.g., 255.255.255.255).

Intranet A network, or collection of networks, that uses Internet standards but is restricted to the members of a particular group or organization. *See also* network.

IP address *See* Internet Protocol address.

Keyword(s) Words entered into a search form to locate matching content on the Web. *See also* search form.

Links Enable the user to open related Web pages by clicking them with the mouse.

List box Lets the user make a selection from a list of pre-defined choices. It has the advantage of always accepting valid input by eliminating the possibility of entering incorrect data.

Listing newsgroups This option in Collabra allows the user to see the names of the discussion groups available on the current news server.

Load a Web page Refers to the process of opening a Web page. *See also* hypertext link.

Location maps and directories Type of search tool on the Web that provides graphics and lists that organize Web sites geographically.

Location text box Displays the URL of the current Web page appearing in the document window. *See also* Uniform Resource Locator (URL).

Location-oriented search A search method often conducted using maps. This method is best used when attempting to locate Web sites in a specific geographical area. *See also* Web site, map.

Map A search tool that displays locations of Web sites geographically. This type of search tool works well when searching for Web sites in a particular geographical region.

Menu bar Displays the names of the menus that contain Netscape Navigator commands. Clicking a menu name on the menu bar displays a list of commands from which you can choose.

Messenger *See* Netscape Messenger.

Meta search engines Single forms for querying multiple indices simultaneously when searching the Web.

My Channels A personalized list of subscriptions to channels and Web sites.

Navigate   To move between Web sites.

Navigation toolbar   A collection of buttons and controls to help the user easily maneuver around the Web.

Navigator   *See* Netscape Navigator 4.

Netcaster   *See* Netscape Netcaster.

Netcaster window   The set of controls used to subscribe and customize channel and Webtop delivery.

Netscape Calendar   An enterprise-wide scheduling program that searches for open times in personal schedules on local and remote servers to coordinate meeting times and available resources.

Netscape Collabra   An enhanced newsgroup reader that provides public (Internet) or private (intranet) discussion forums.

Netscape Conference   A real-time audio communication program that enables the user to speak with another person over the Internet or within an intranet.

Netscape Messenger   E-mail client, or program, for sending and receiving electronic messages.

Netscape Navigator 4   The newest Web browser developed by Netscape Communications Corporation. *See also* Web browser.

Netscape Netcaster   A program that lets the user select, or subscribe to, channels of personalized information automatically delivered to the desktop. *See also* Webcasting, Push technology.

Netscape Composer   An editor for creating Web pages that provides easy-to-use features to modify, format, enhance, and publish Web pages or even an entire Web presentation. *See also* Web presentation.

Network   Two or more computers connected together in order to exchange data and share resources.

Newsgroup   A collection of Internet users meeting electronically to discuss a particular topic of interest by posting and exchanging messages. Also known as a discussion group.

Online libraries   Provide collections of publications in an electronic form easily accessible to users.

Online storefront   A place on the Web where a company markets its products and services. *See also* virtual shopping malls, virtual storefront.

People finders   Search tools for the Web that locate people.

Personal toolbar   A customizable toolbar that contains Internet shortcuts to a user's favorite sites.

Plug-ins   Programs designed to work with Netscape Navigator to allow the viewing of multimedia content on the Web.

Progress bar   Displays important information about the current operation, such as the percentage loaded of a Web page's layout and graphics. *See also* load a Web page.

Protocol   A communication standard (e.g., HyperText Transfer Protocol) to ensure that different computers can successfully exchange information.

Push technology   A means to deliver personalized information automatically to a user's desktop. *See also* Webcasting.

Relevancy scores   Ratings of how closely search results match a query to a search engine.

Scroll bar   A bar—appearing at the bottom and/or right edge of a window that contains more content than can be displayed at one time—that lets the user move up and down the page, or right and left, to view the entire document. *See also* horizontal scroll bar, vertical scroll bar.

Scroll box   A small square-shaped control, located in the vertical and horizontal scroll bars, that lets the user quickly move through a long document and indicates the relative position in the document. *See also* horizontal scroll bar, vertical scroll bar.

Search engine   A Web site that uses entries in a search form to scan for relevant information stored in an index of the Web. *See also* search form.

Search form   A Web page that enables the user to specify what information a search engine should look for. *See also* search engine.

Secured site   Refers to any Web site that uses encrypted transmissions and takes other appropriate measures to ensure the protection of sensitive information such as credit card information. *See also* security indicator.

Security indicator   A door key icon that indicates if the information you are viewing is secured. If the door key icon displays in blue, then the information is secured; if the door key is broken and displays in gray, then the Web document is not secured. *See also* secured site.

Status indicator   The Netscape Communications company logo that appears in the upper-right corner of the Navigator window and animates as a new Web page is loading. When the status indicator stops moving, the page loading process is complete. *See also* load a Web page.

Strand   A series of linked Web pages. *See also* hypertext links.

Internet

Subject directories Search tools on the Web that are grouped and arranged by topic.

Subject-oriented catalog A search tool that lists topics alphabetically from A–Z to facilitate browsing. This type of search tool is effective in finding general or broad information. *See also* subject-oriented search.

Subject-oriented search Type of search effective in finding general or broad information. *See also* subject-oriented catalog.

Surfing the Web Refers to the activity of randomly or intentionally selecting the links found in Web pages to travel, or navigate, about the Web. *See also* hypertext links.

Title bar Displays the title of the current Web page at the top of the Navigator application window.

Toolbar Contains icons that function as shortcuts to frequently used Netscape Navigator menu commands.

Top level domain The last letters of a domain name that indicate the category to which a Web site belongs. For example, the global name extension .edu indicates that the Web site is part of the educational domain on the Internet. *See also* global domain.

Uniform Resource Locator (URL) Unique string of text that identifies the location of a Web page on the World Wide Web. *See* address.

Vertical scroll bar Allows the user to quickly move back and forth across a Web page.

Virtual community A site in cyberspace where people gather to discuss topics of mutual interest, make friends, and form relationships.

Virtual reality A three-dimensional interactive environment.

Virtual shopping malls Groups of online storefronts where companies market their goods and services on the World Wide Web. *See also* online storefront.

Virtual storefront A Web site established by a company that wants to create a unique and individual business, or commercial, presence on the Web. *See also* Web site.

VRML Virtual Reality Modeling Language, a programming language used to create three-dimensional environments on the Web. *See also* virtual reality.

W3 Another name for the World Wide Web—a vast series of electronic documents called Web pages or Web documents that are linked together over the Internet. Also referred to as the Web. *See also* Web.

Web, The *See* World Wide Web (WWW).

Web address Unique string of text that identifies the location of a Web page on the World Wide Web. Also known as the URL (Uniform Resource Locator) for a Web page or site.

Web browser Computer program that enables users to view and interact with Web sites on the World Wide Web. Web browsers offer easy-to-use point and click environments for quickly accessing information on the Web. *See also* Netscape Navigator 4.

Web document *See* Web page.

Web page A specially formatted file designed for use on the World Wide Web that enables the user to display Web pages in a Web browser. Web pages typically include text, graphics, and links to other Web pages, and sometimes sound and video clips. Also referred to as a Web document. *See also* hypertext links.

Web site One or more computers and software that make Web pages available to World Wide Web users. Also referred to as a Web server.

Webcasting Lets the user subscribe to a channel of information that is automatically delivered to a user's desktop. *See also* Push technology.

Webtop A borderless Web page that displays channel content using your entire computer screen.

World Wide Web (WWW) A vast series of electronic documents called Web pages or Web documents that are linked together over the Internet. Also referred to as The Web and W3. *See also* Web page.

WWW Virtual Library Large subject-oriented catalog on the Web covering a wide range of subjects. *See also* subject-oriented catalog.

Internet

Index

Index

Index